MEN

Photography by Dan Simoneau

Evy

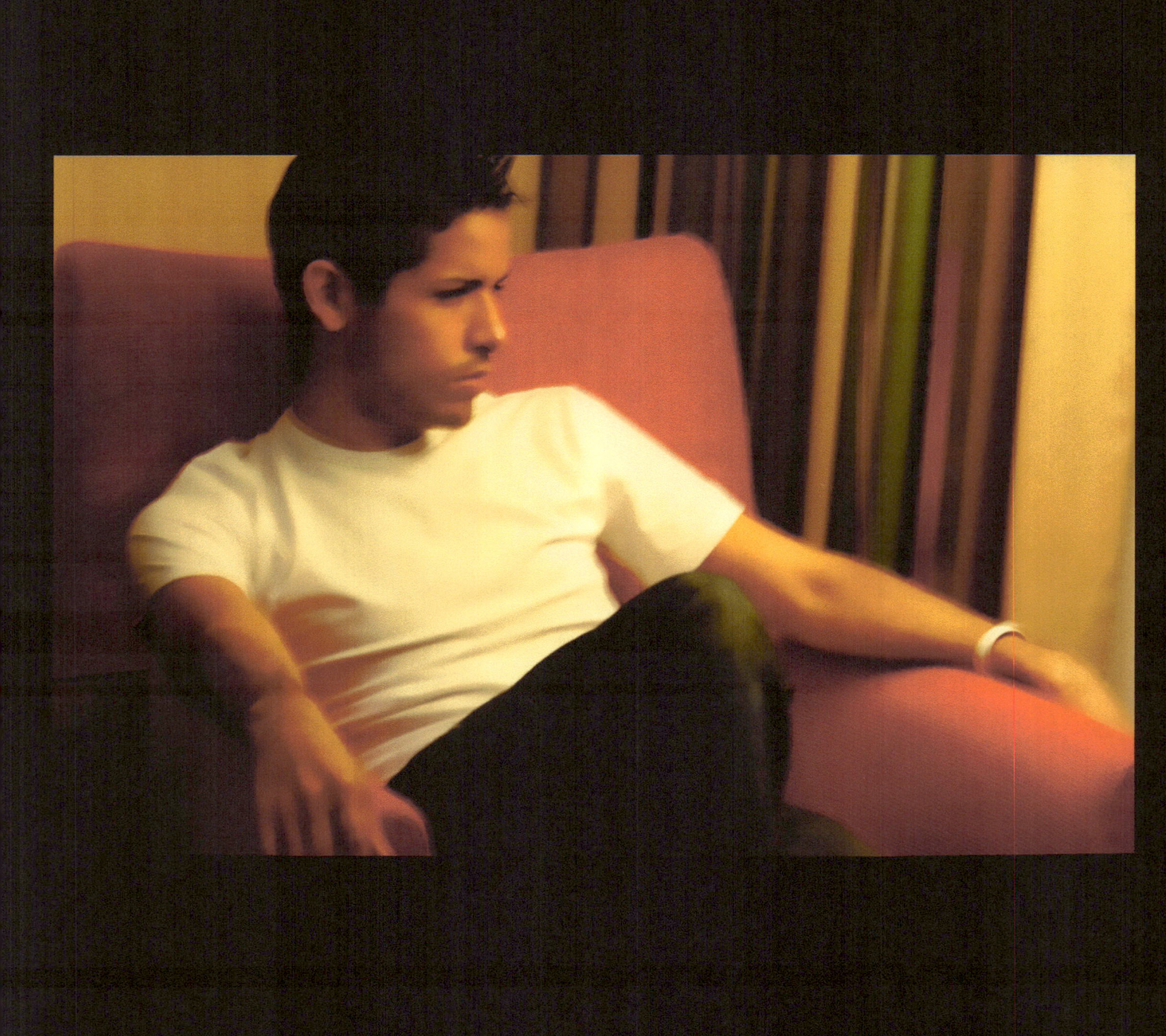

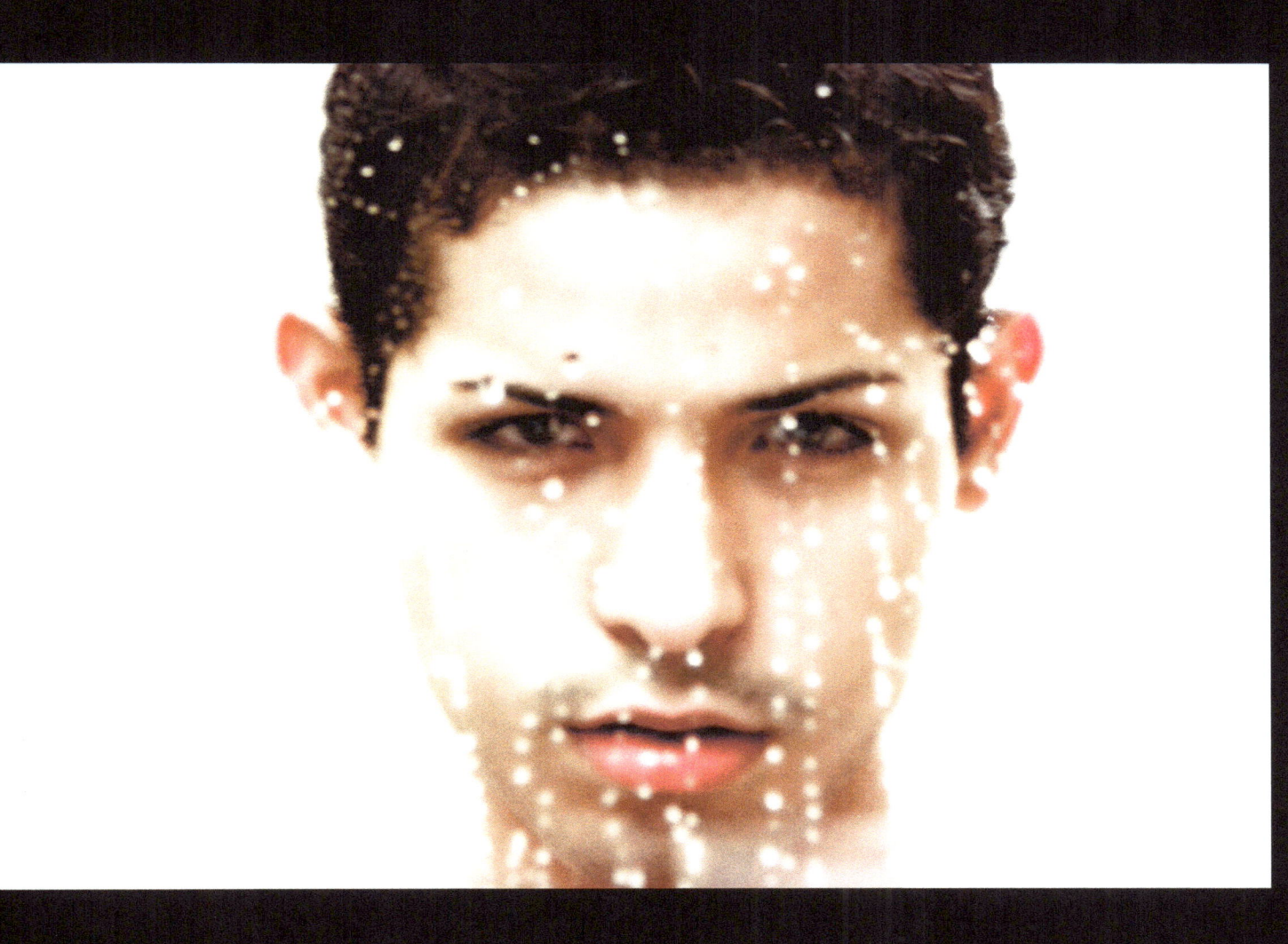

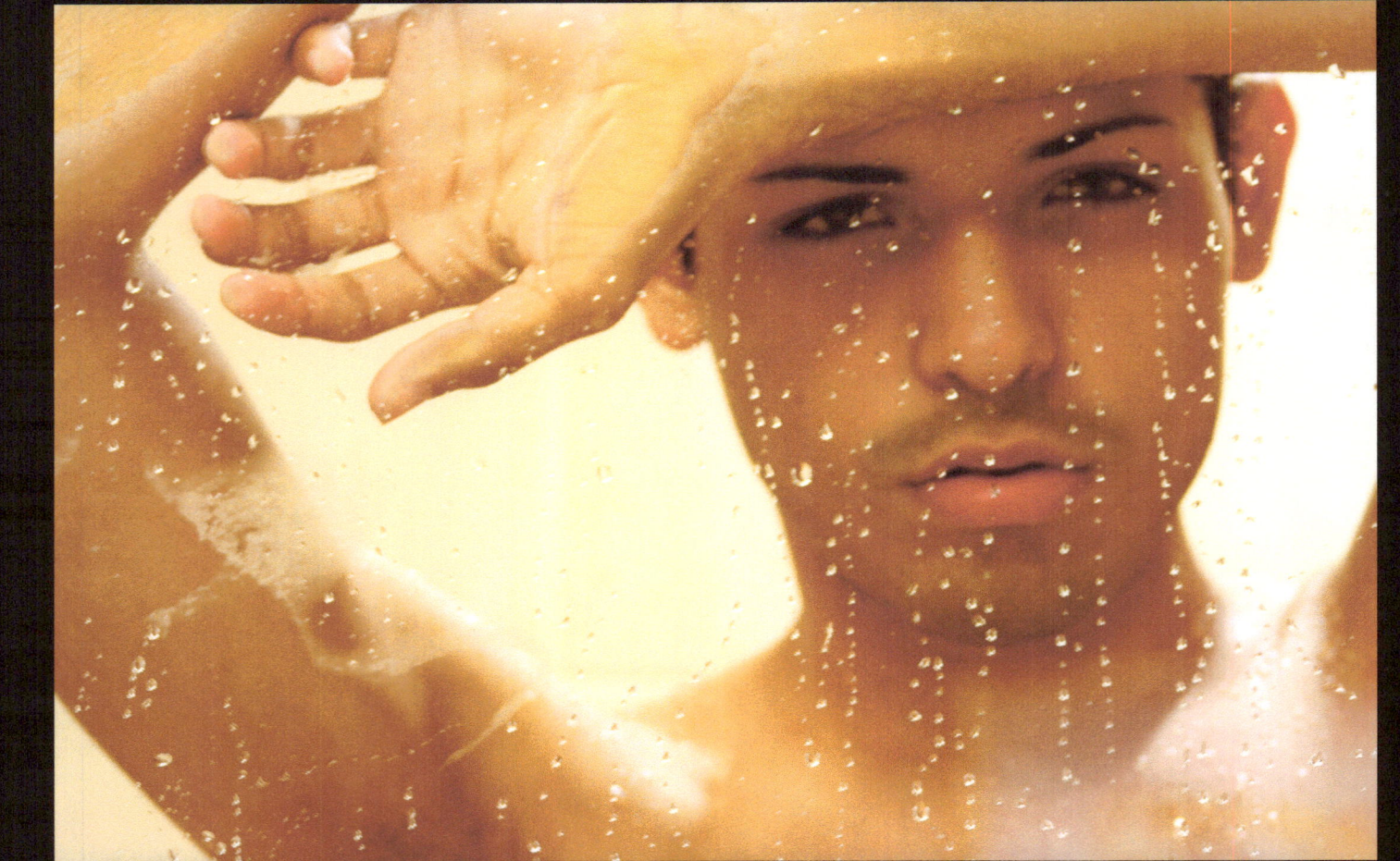

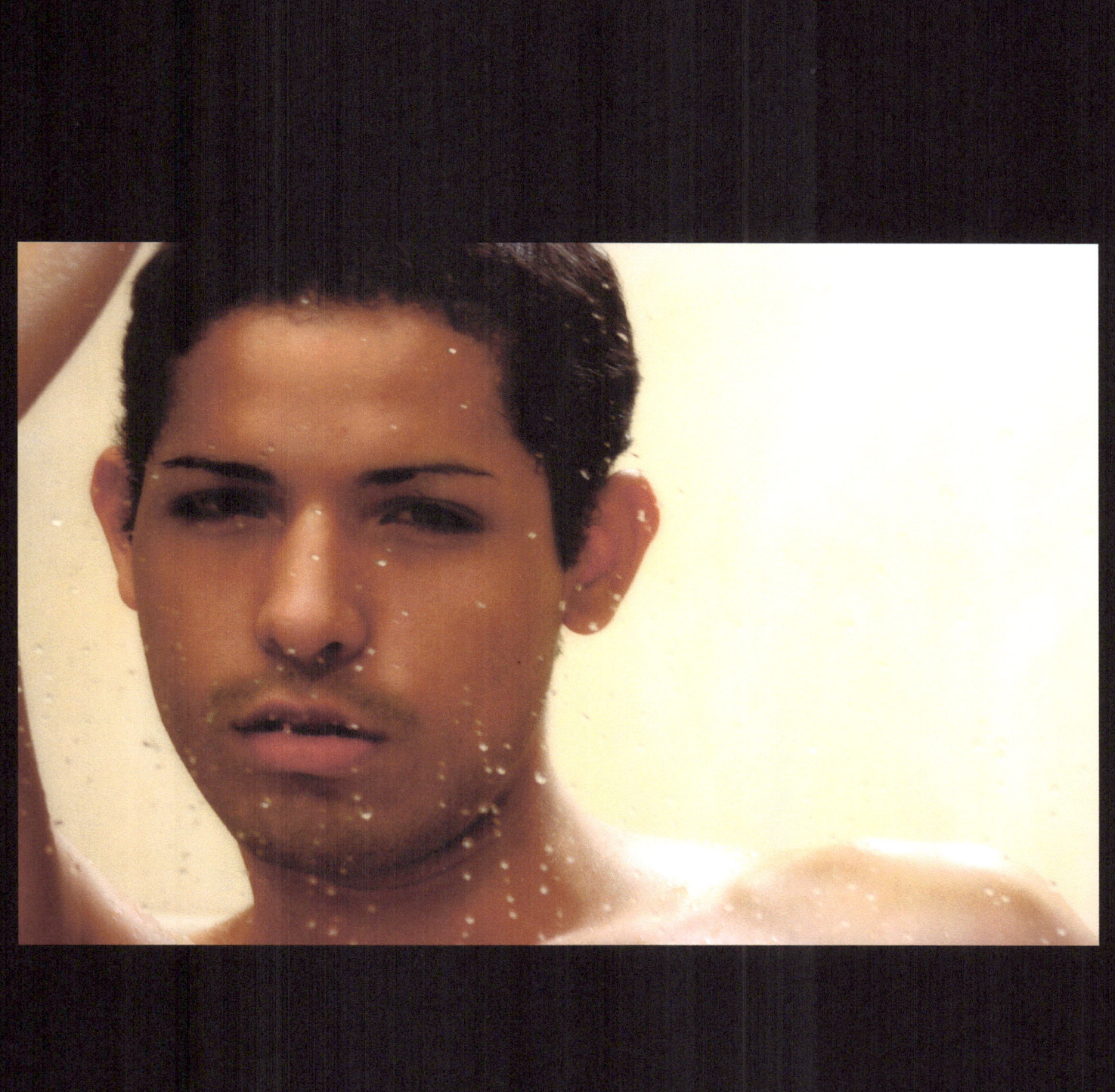

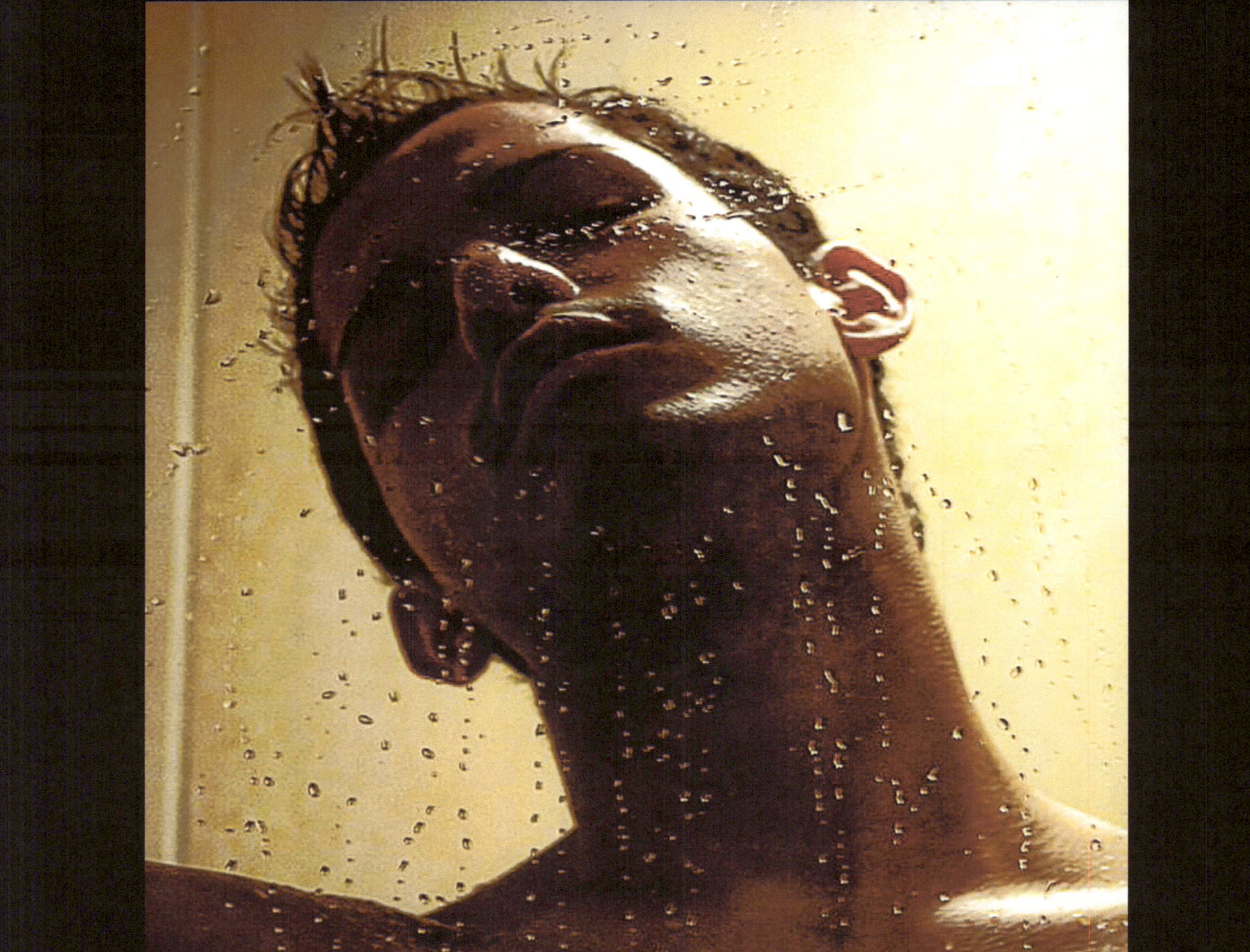

Rafael
(Raffy)

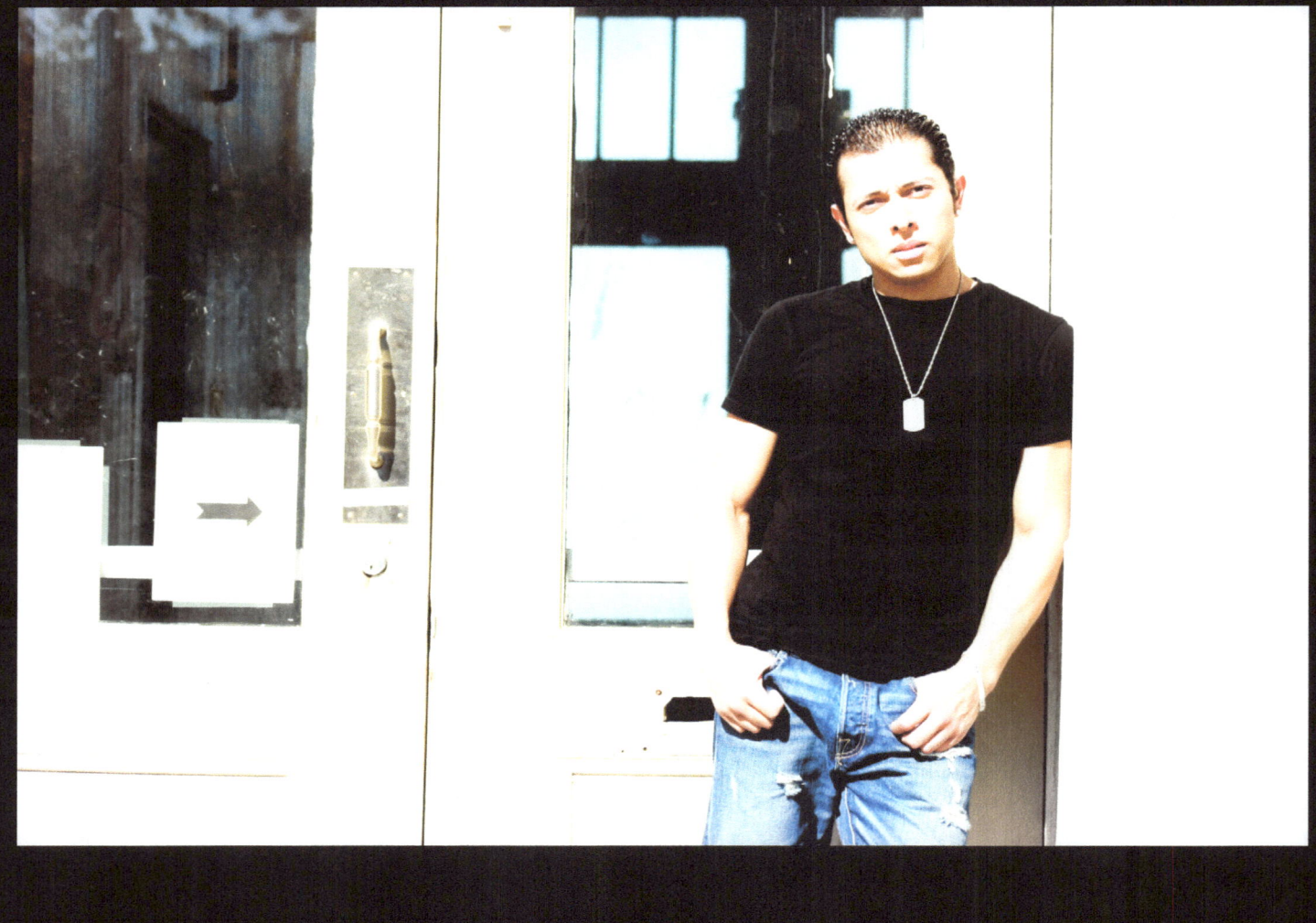

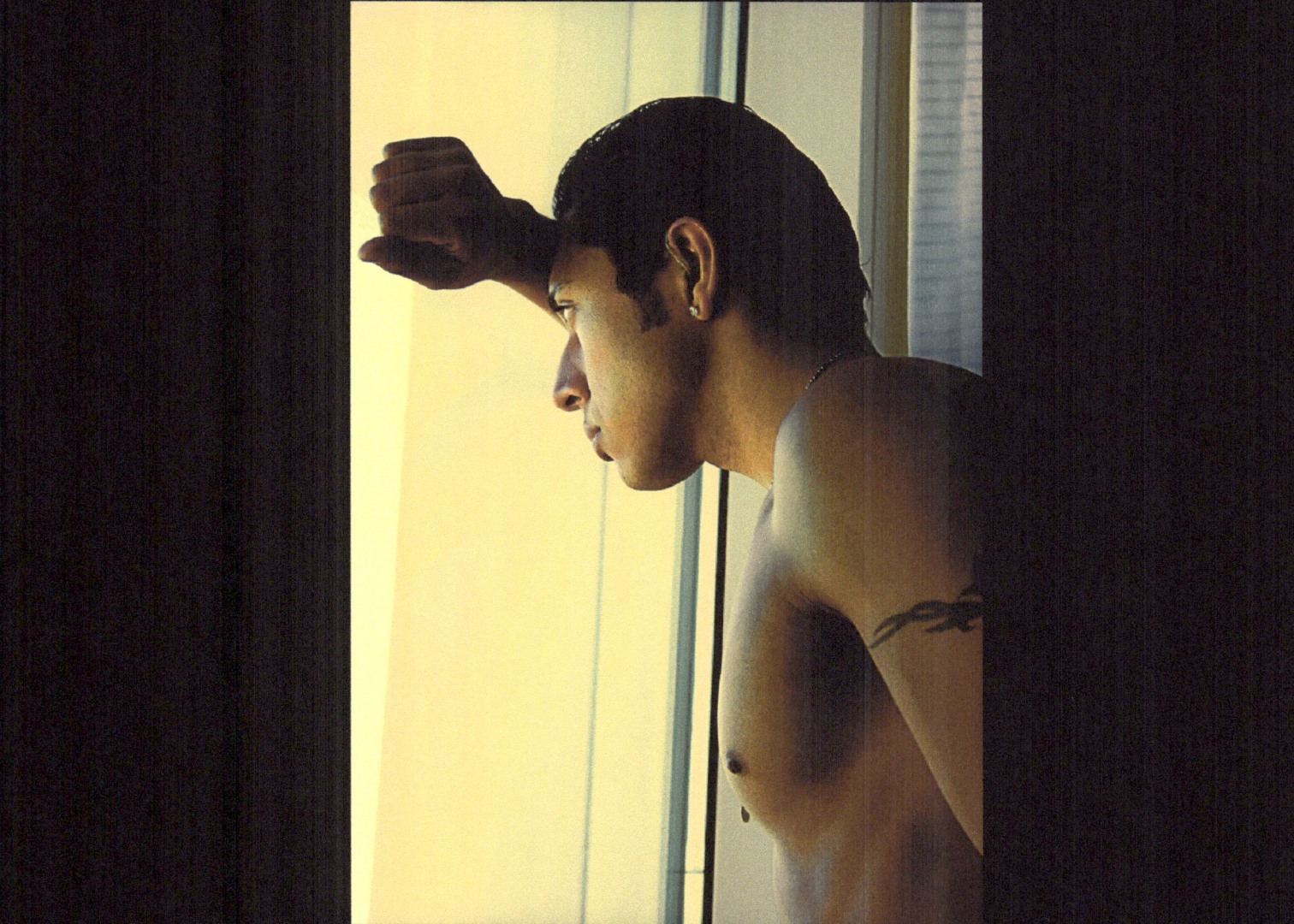

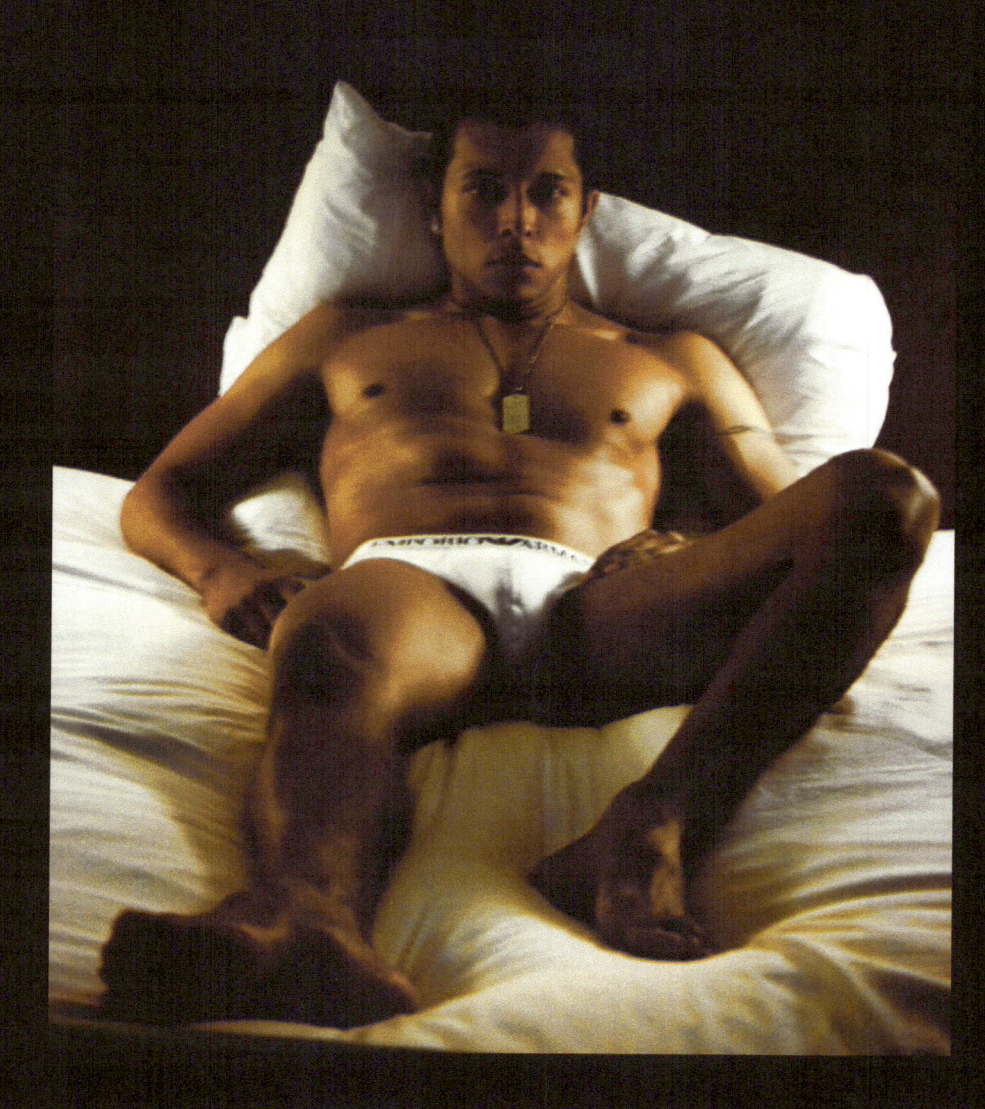

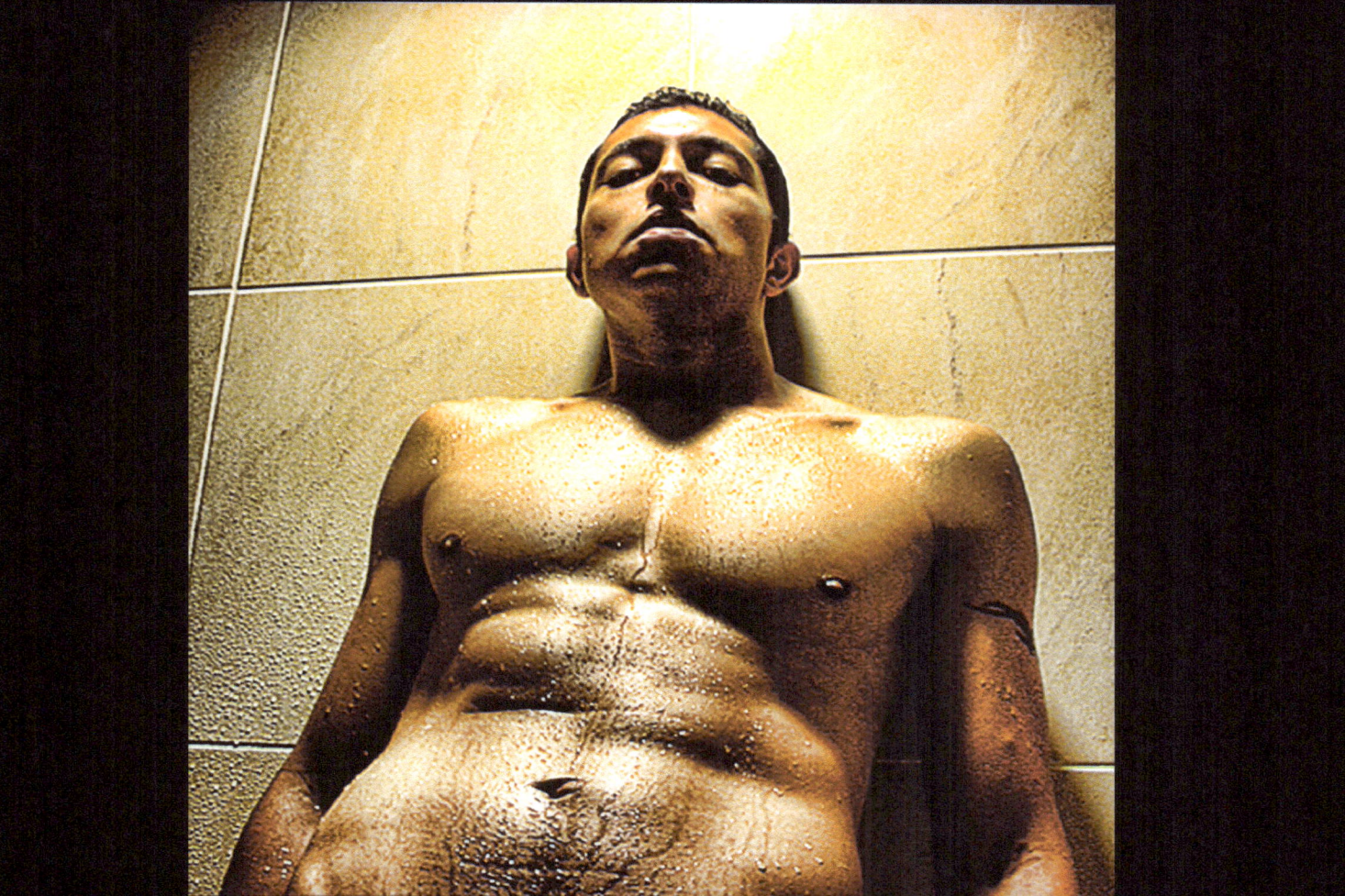

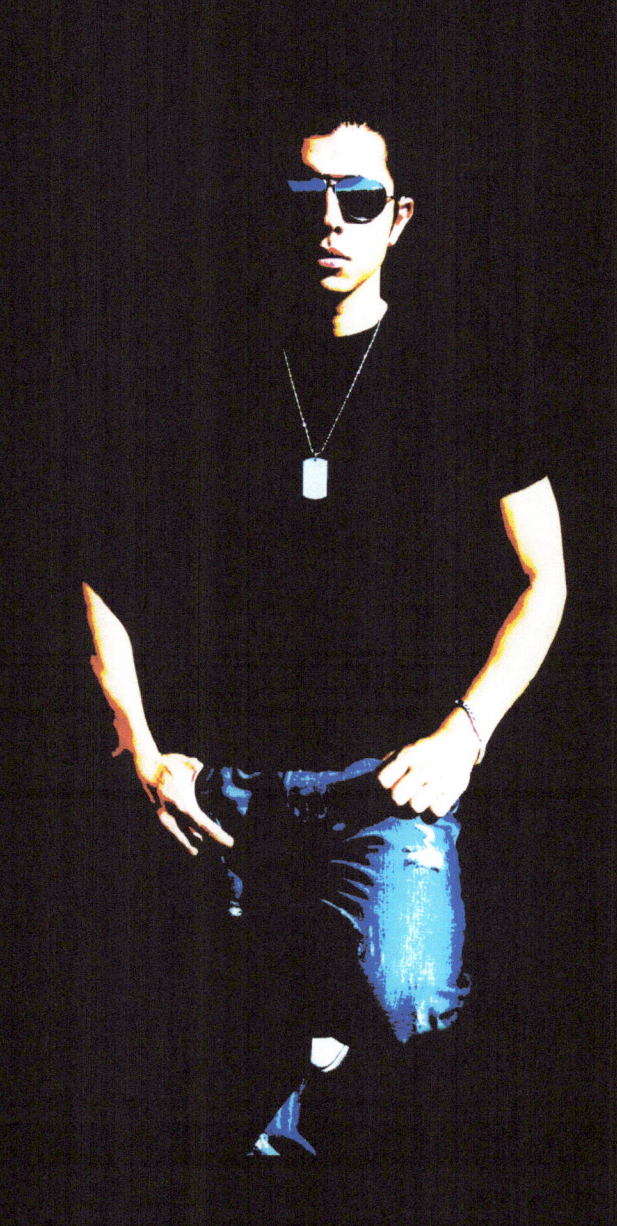

Quincey

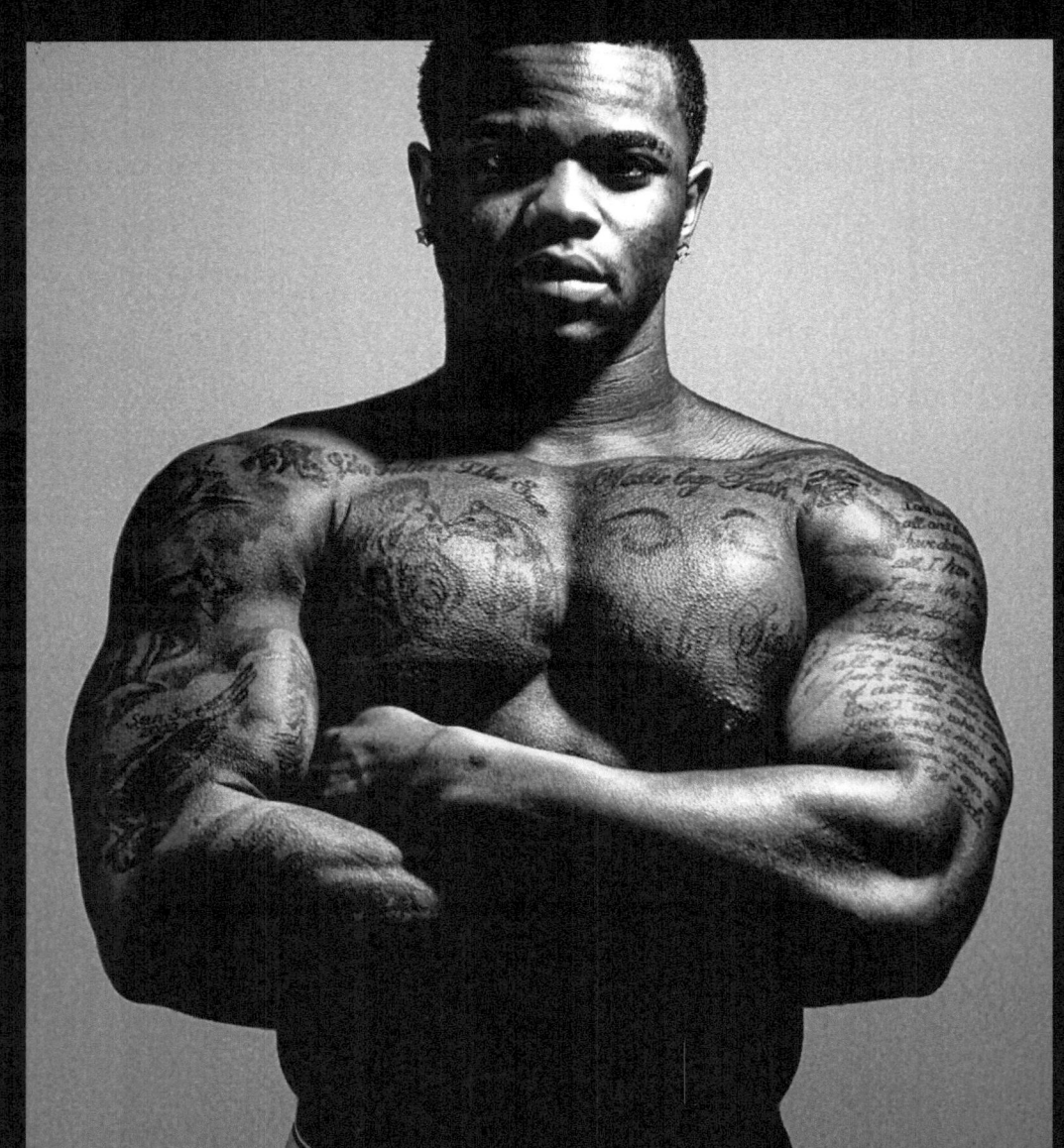

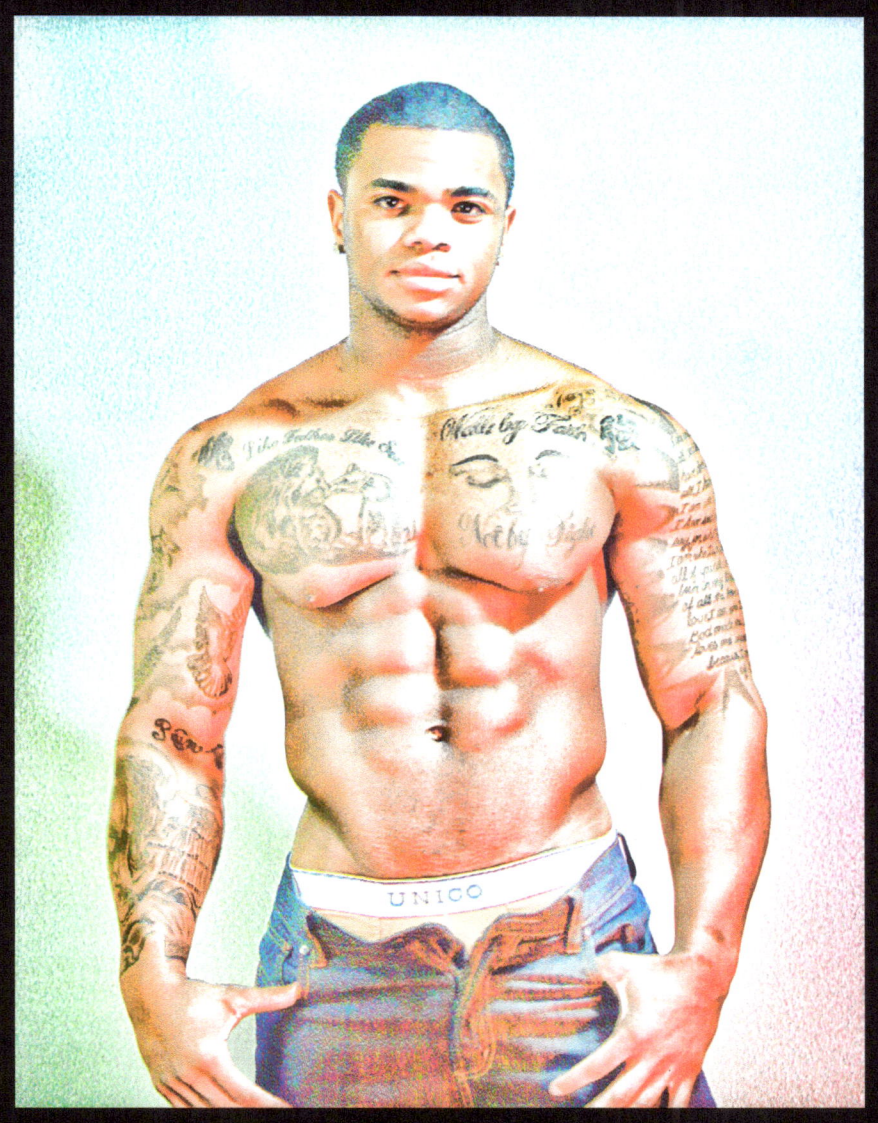

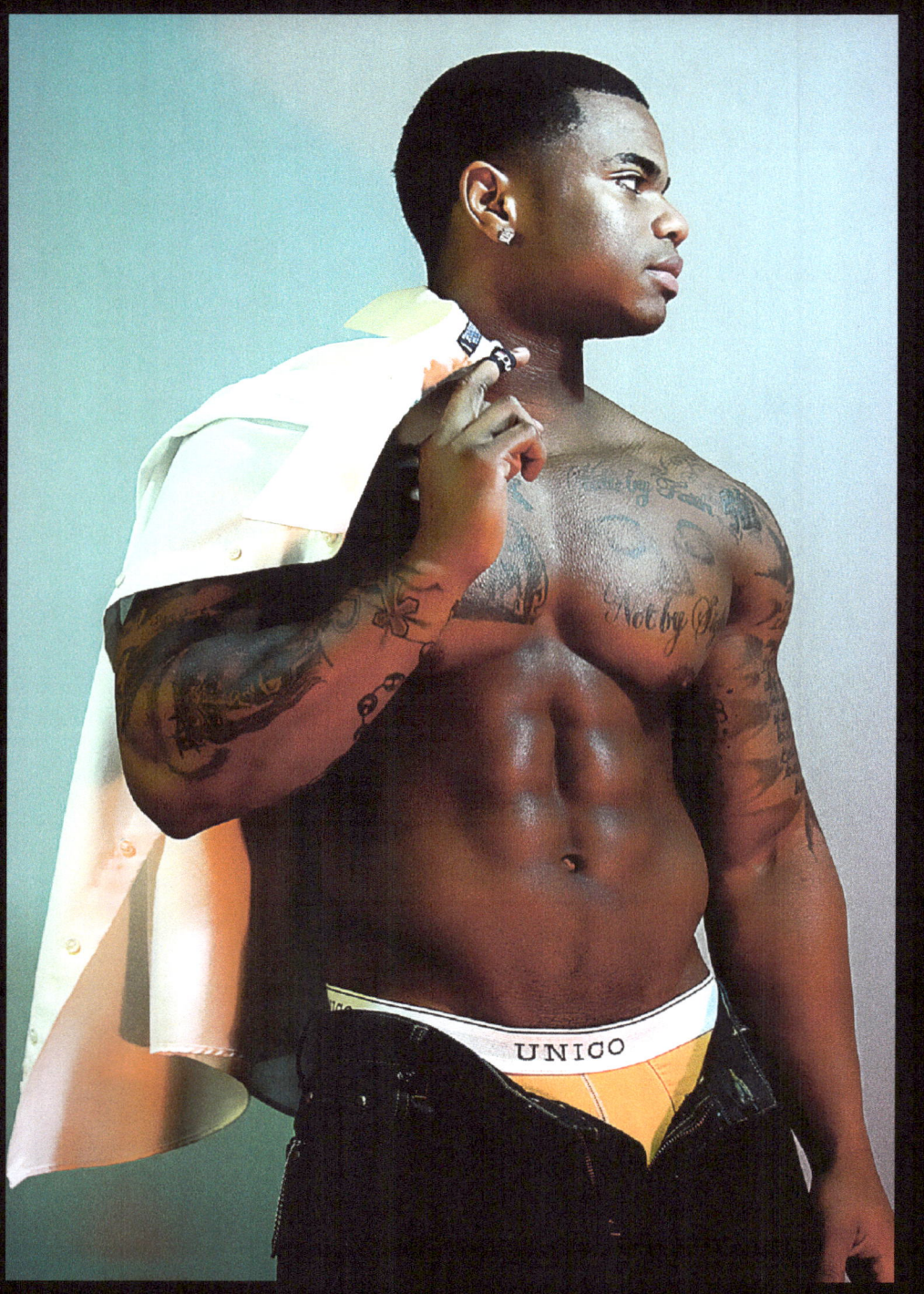

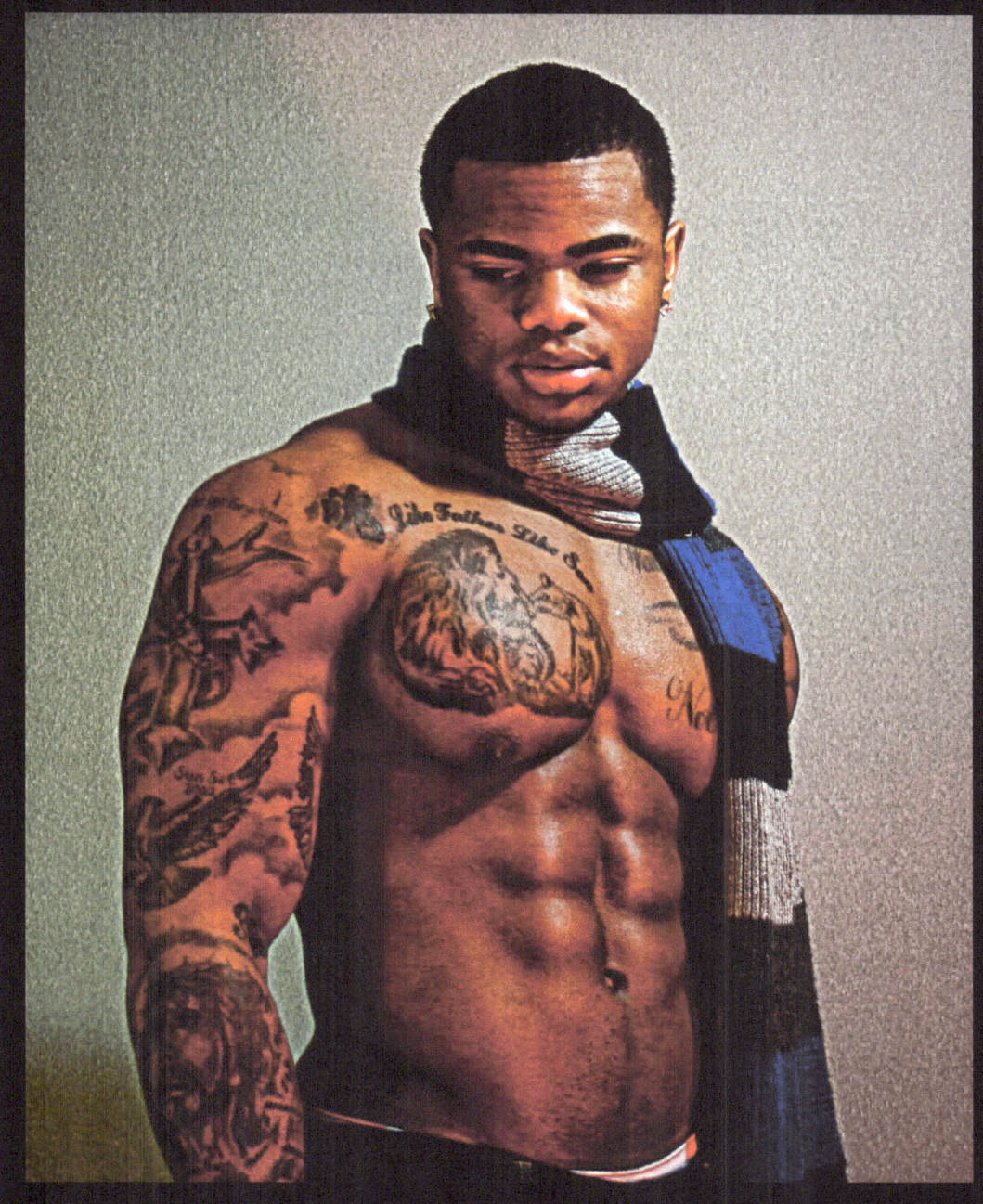

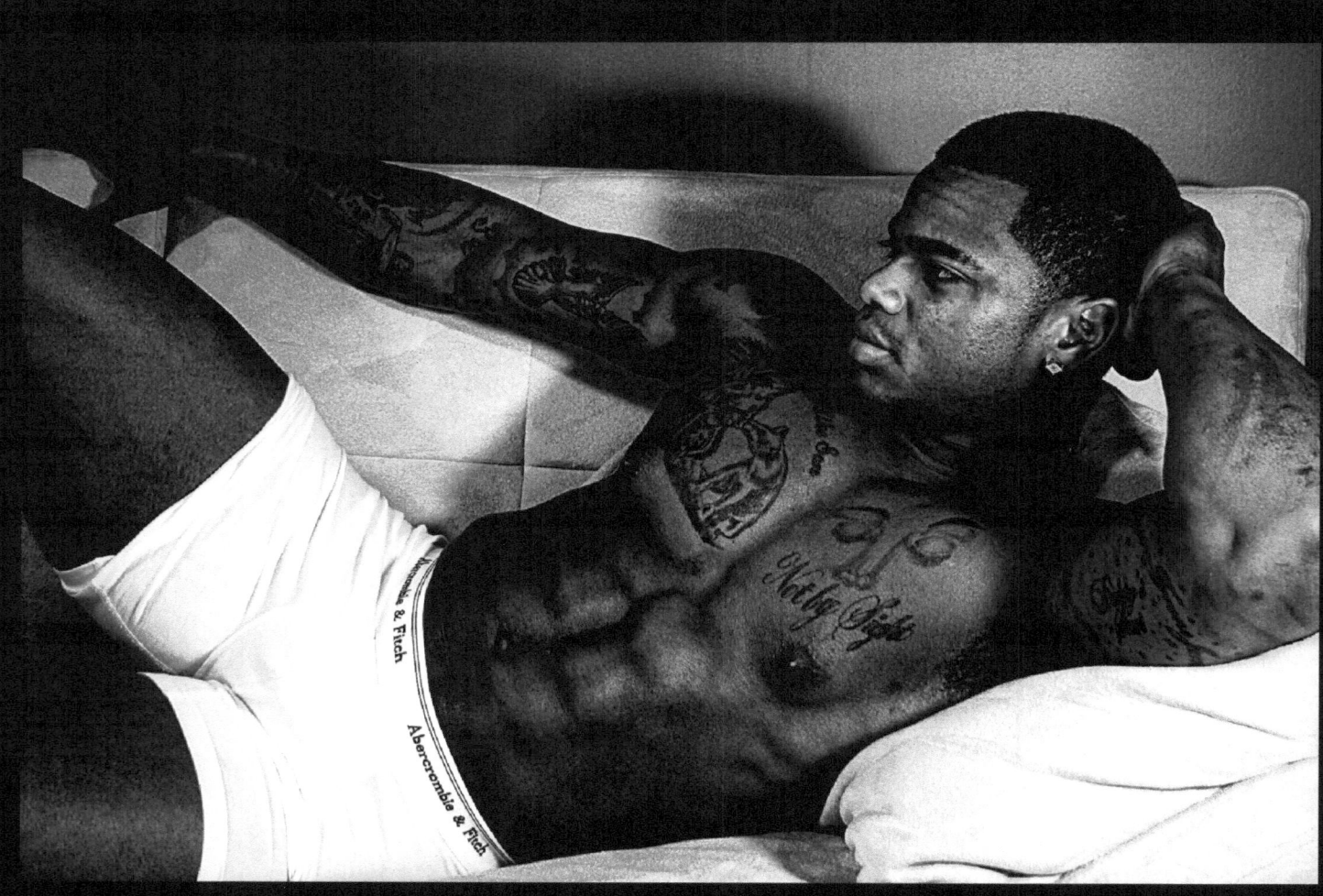

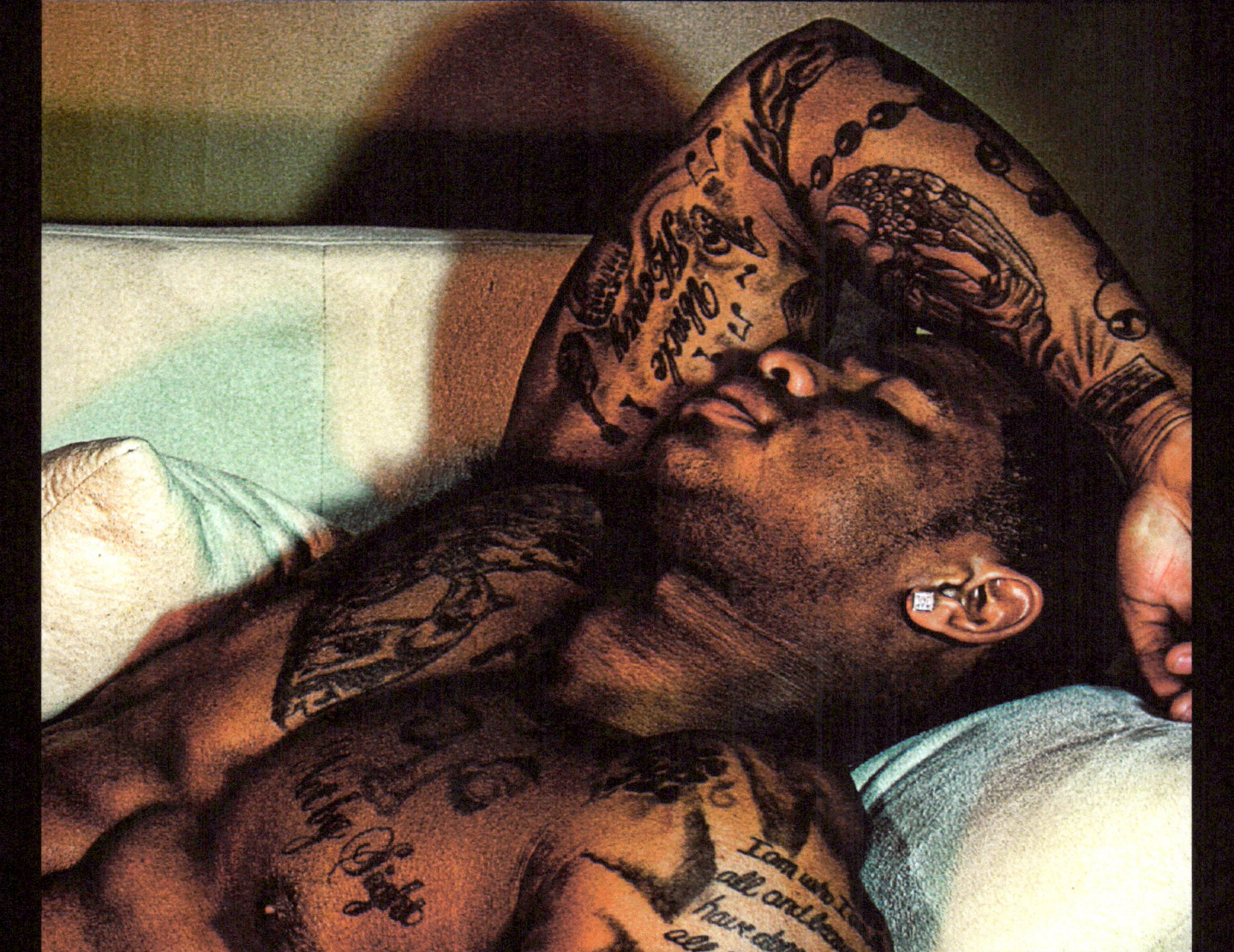

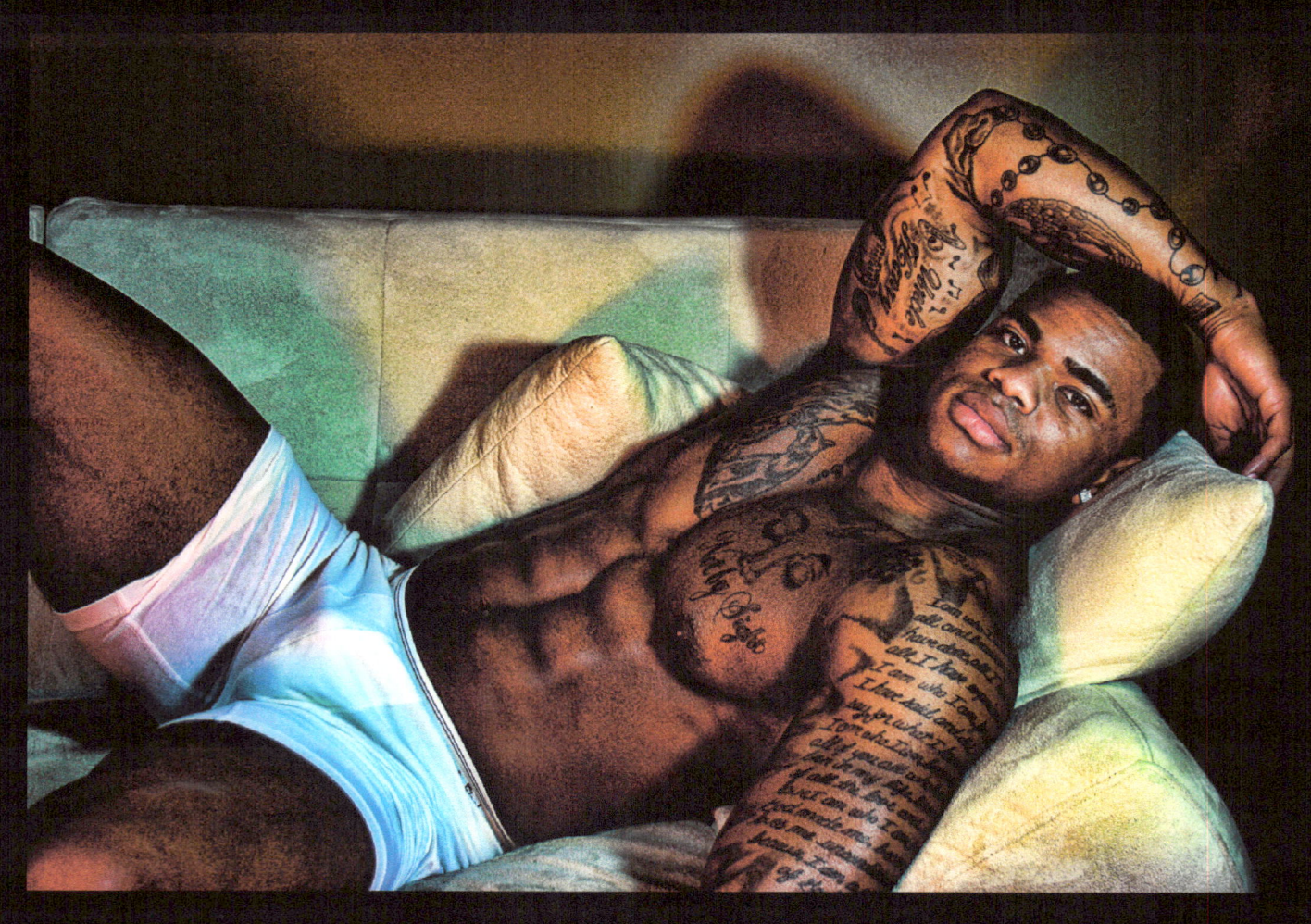

Walter
(Dubya)

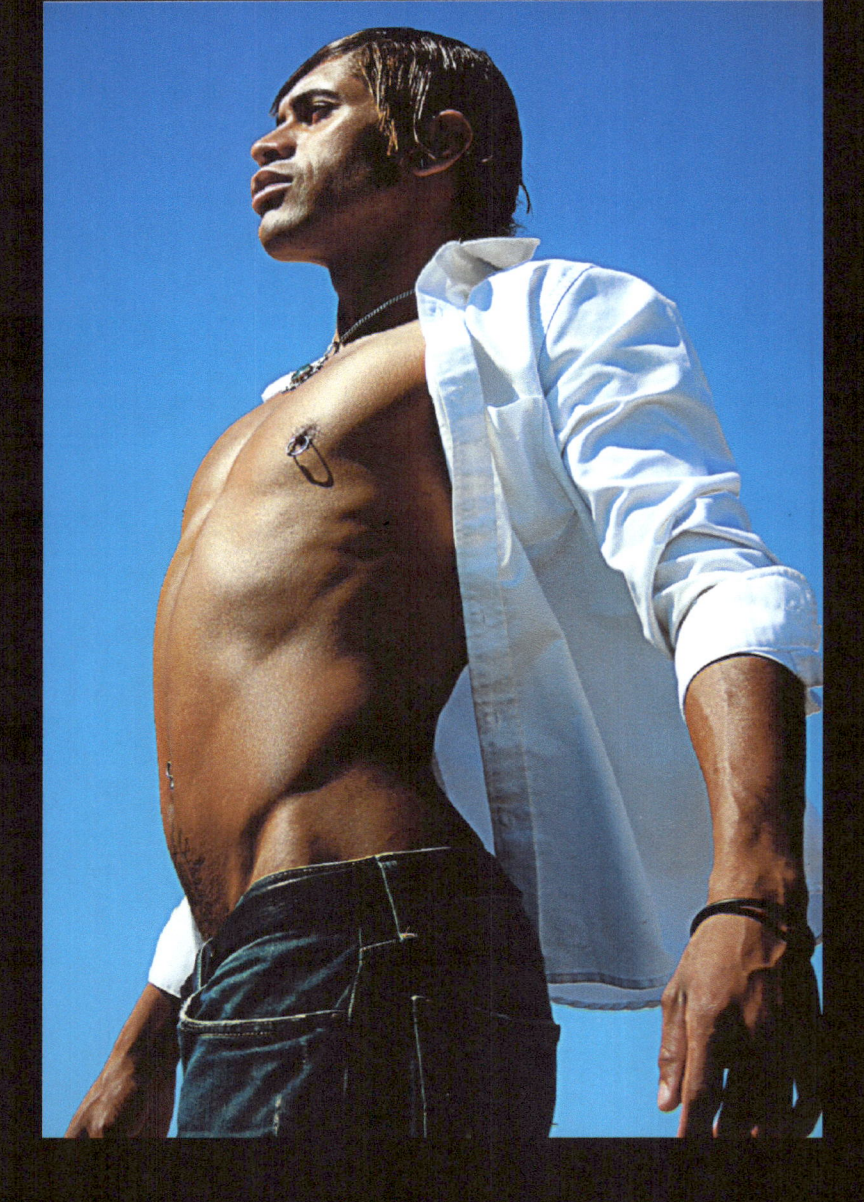

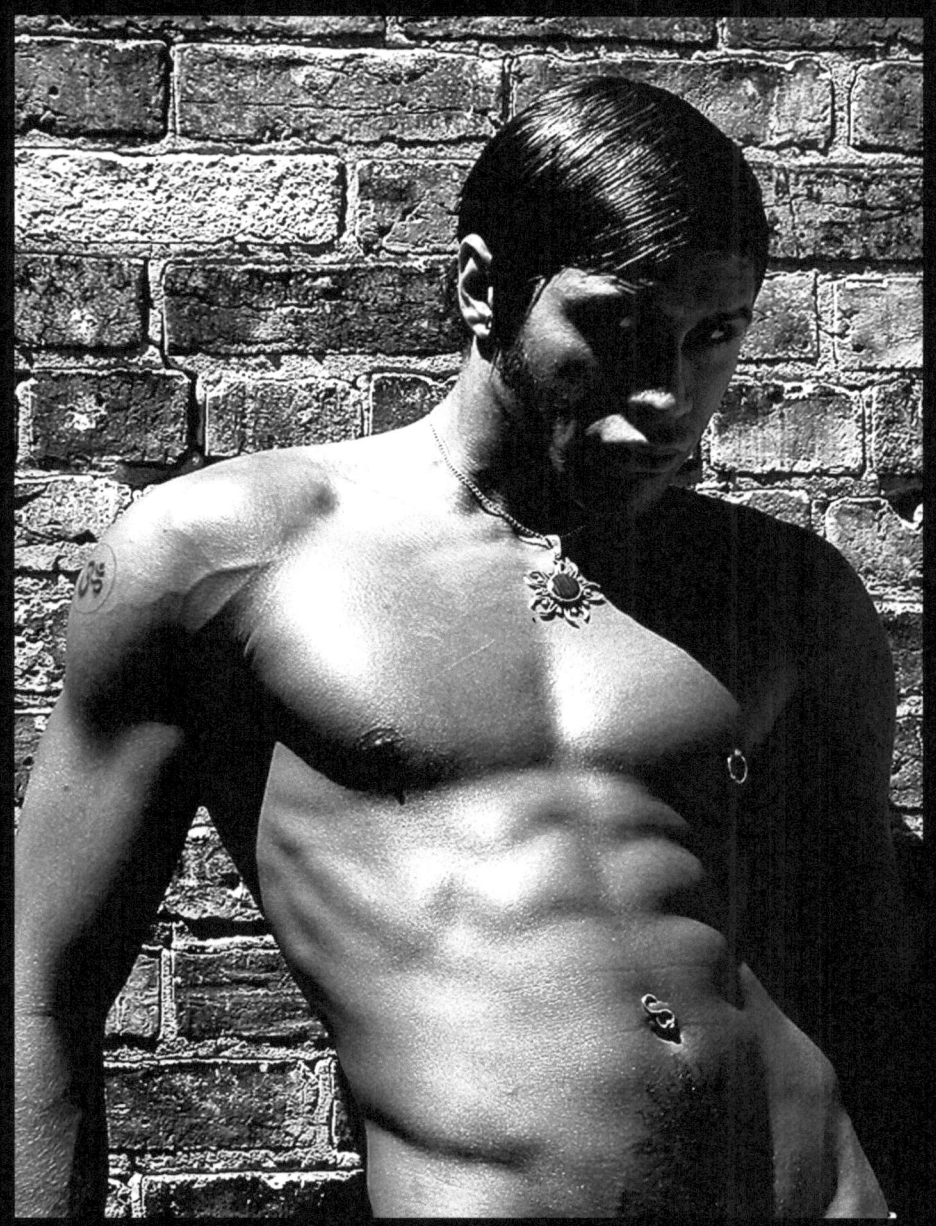

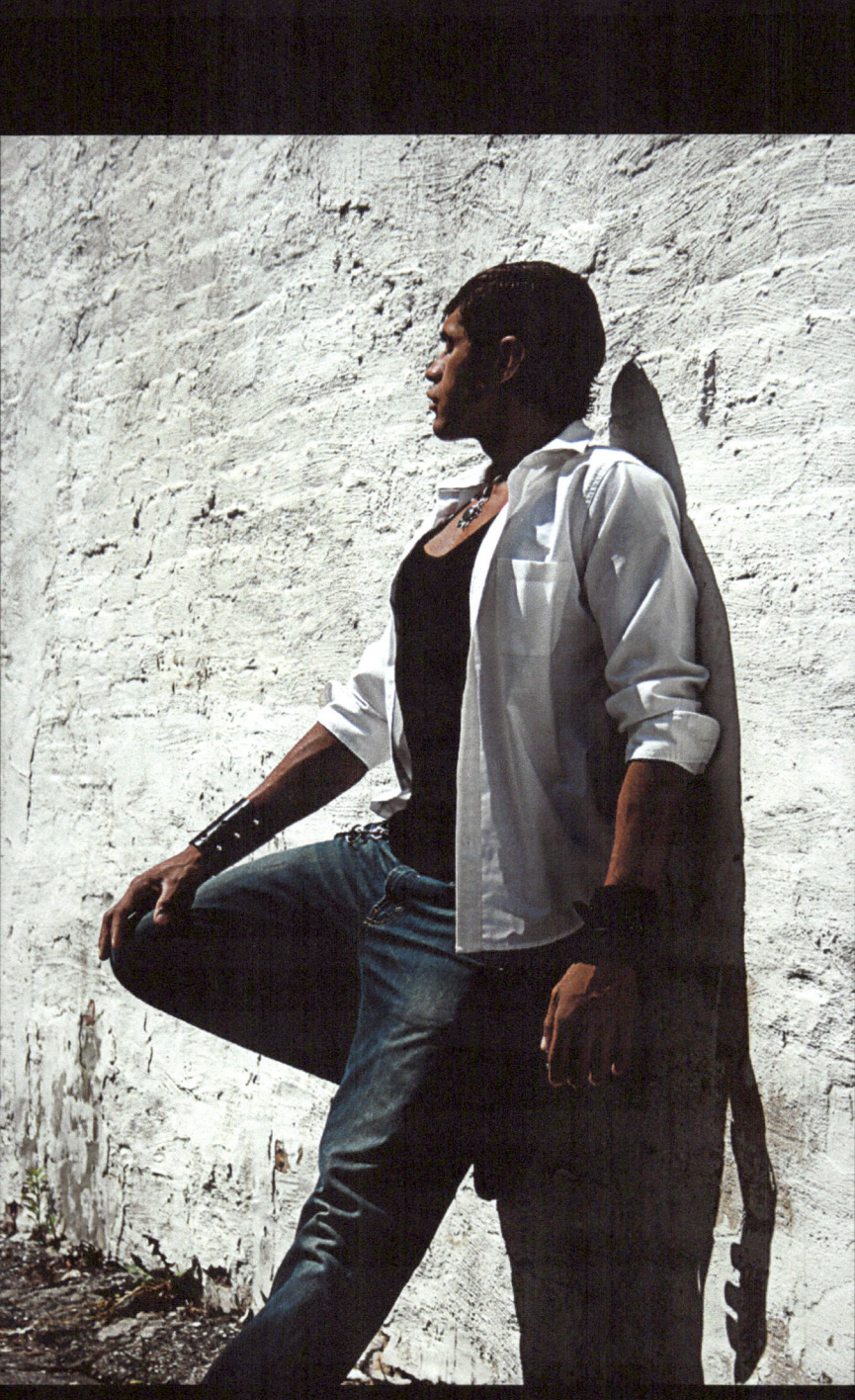

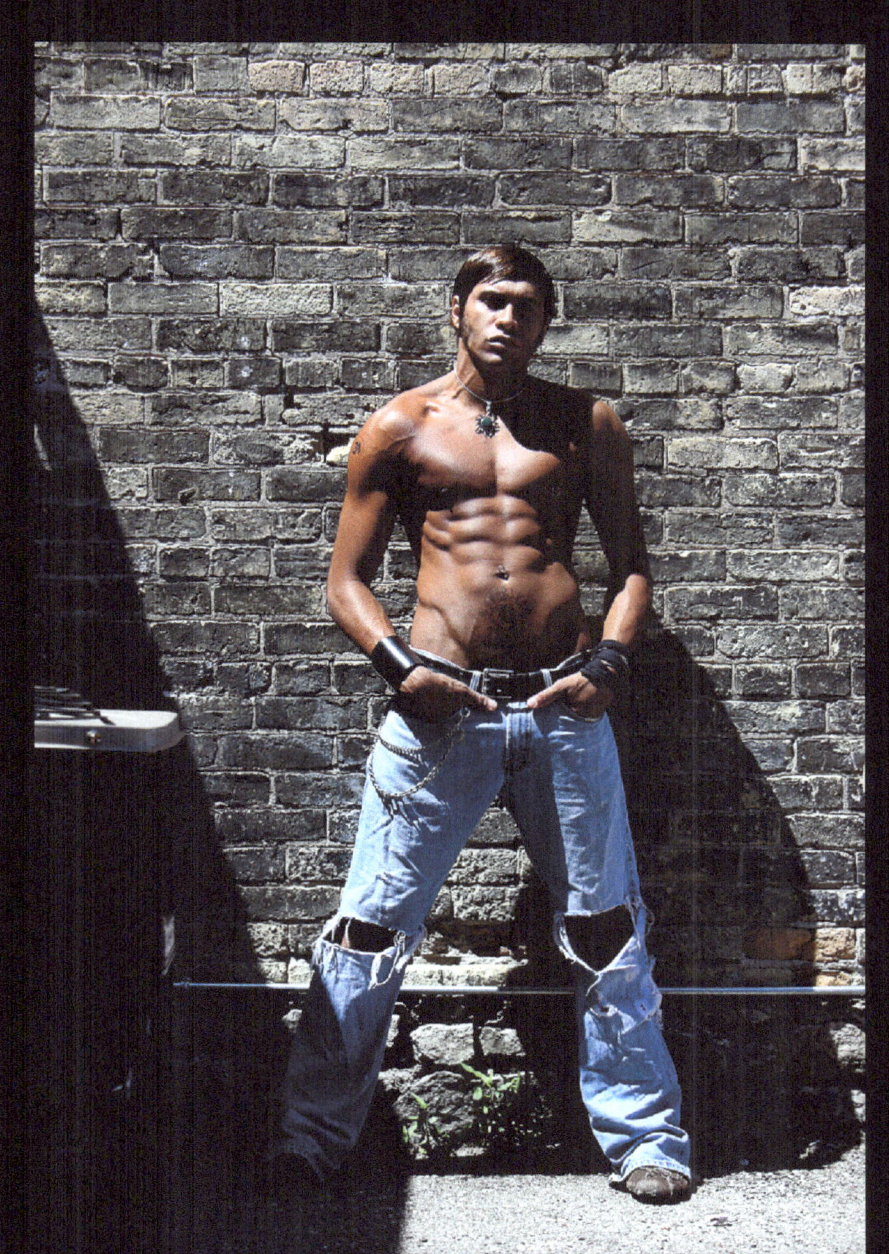

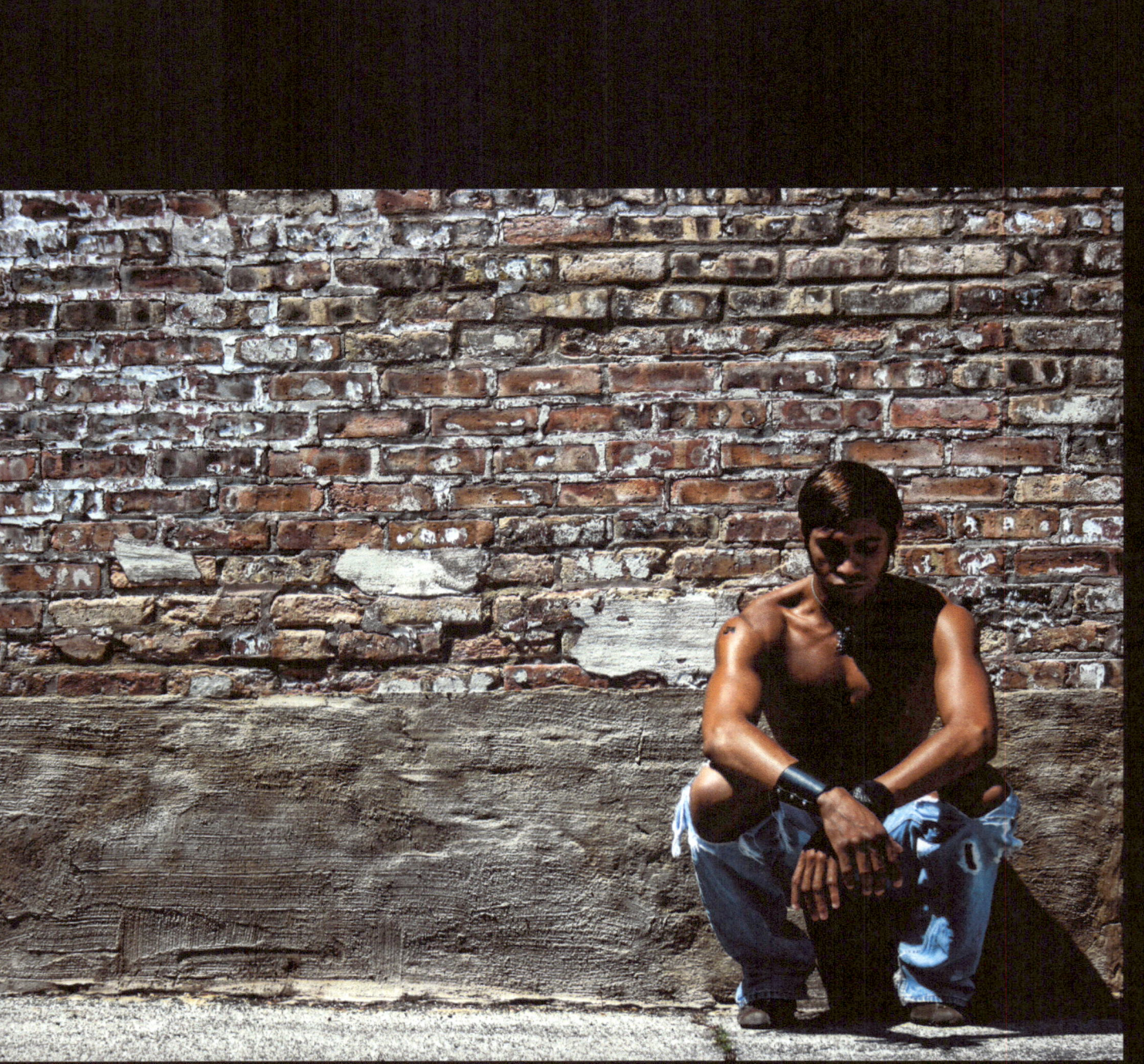

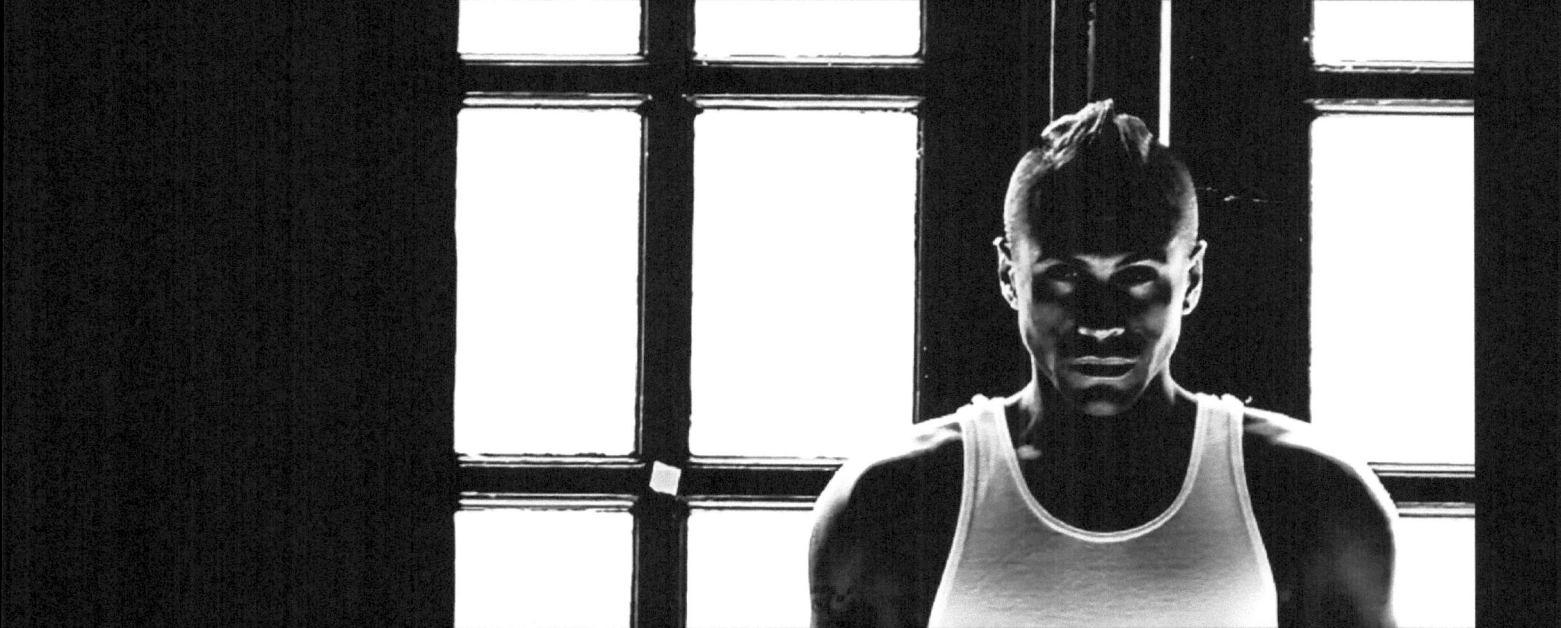

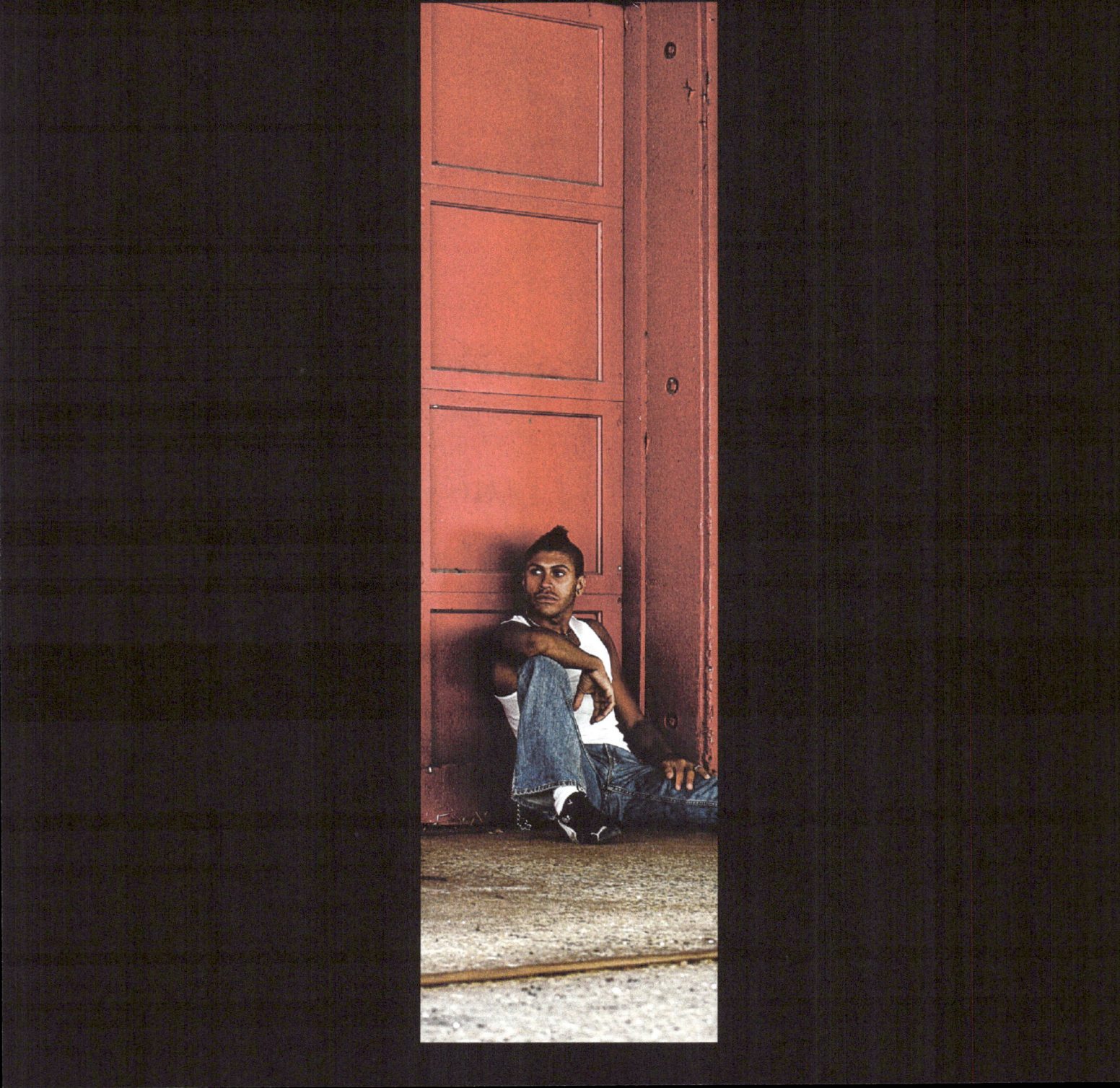

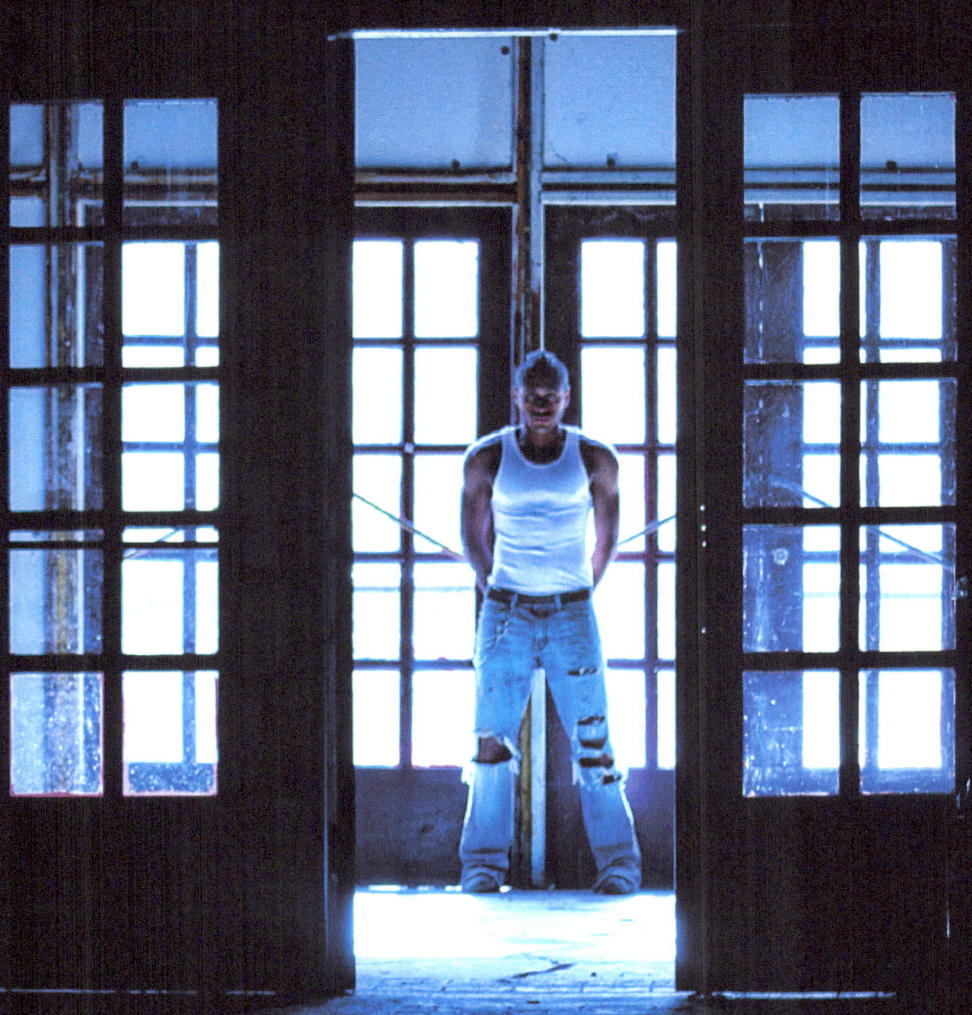

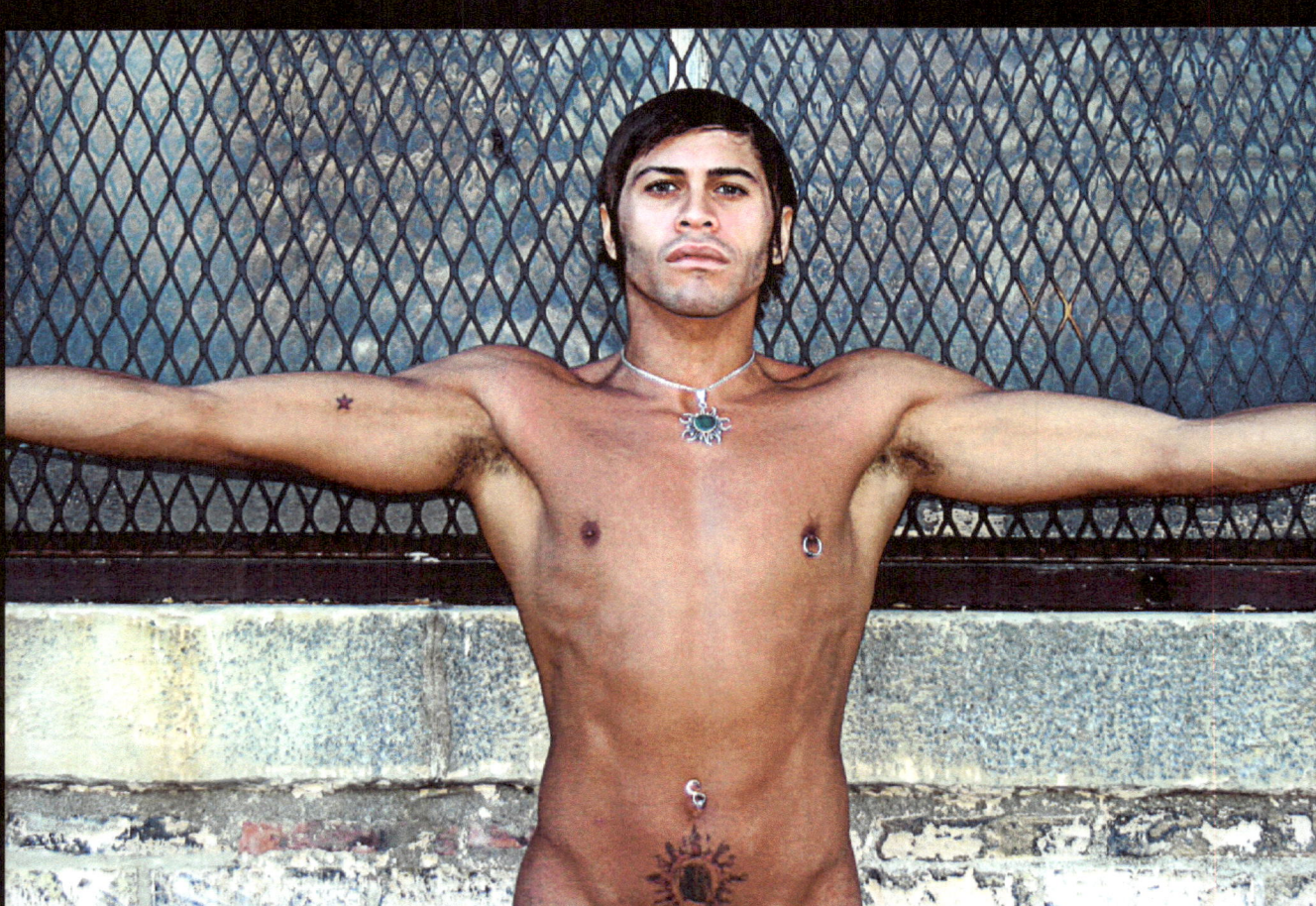

Scott

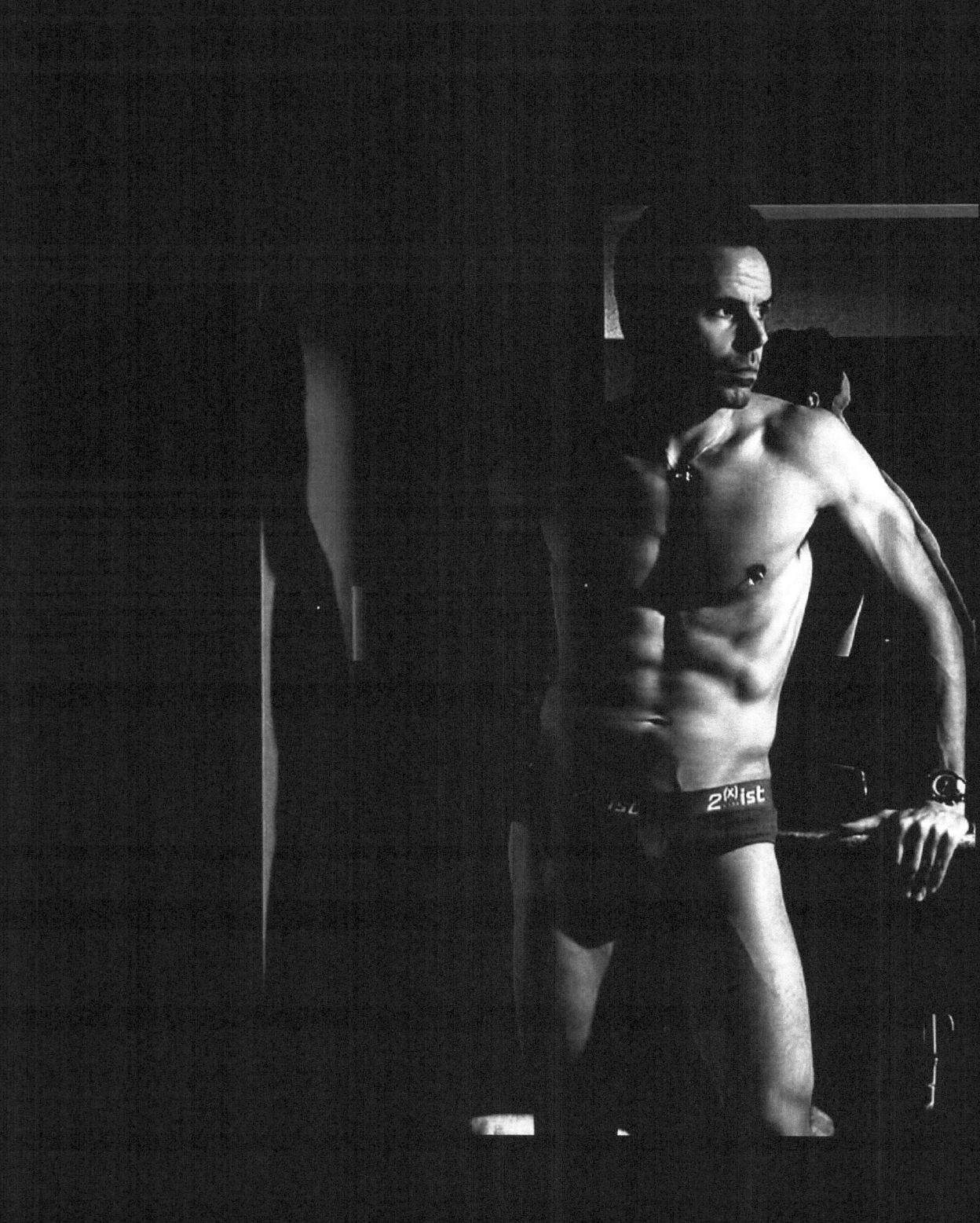

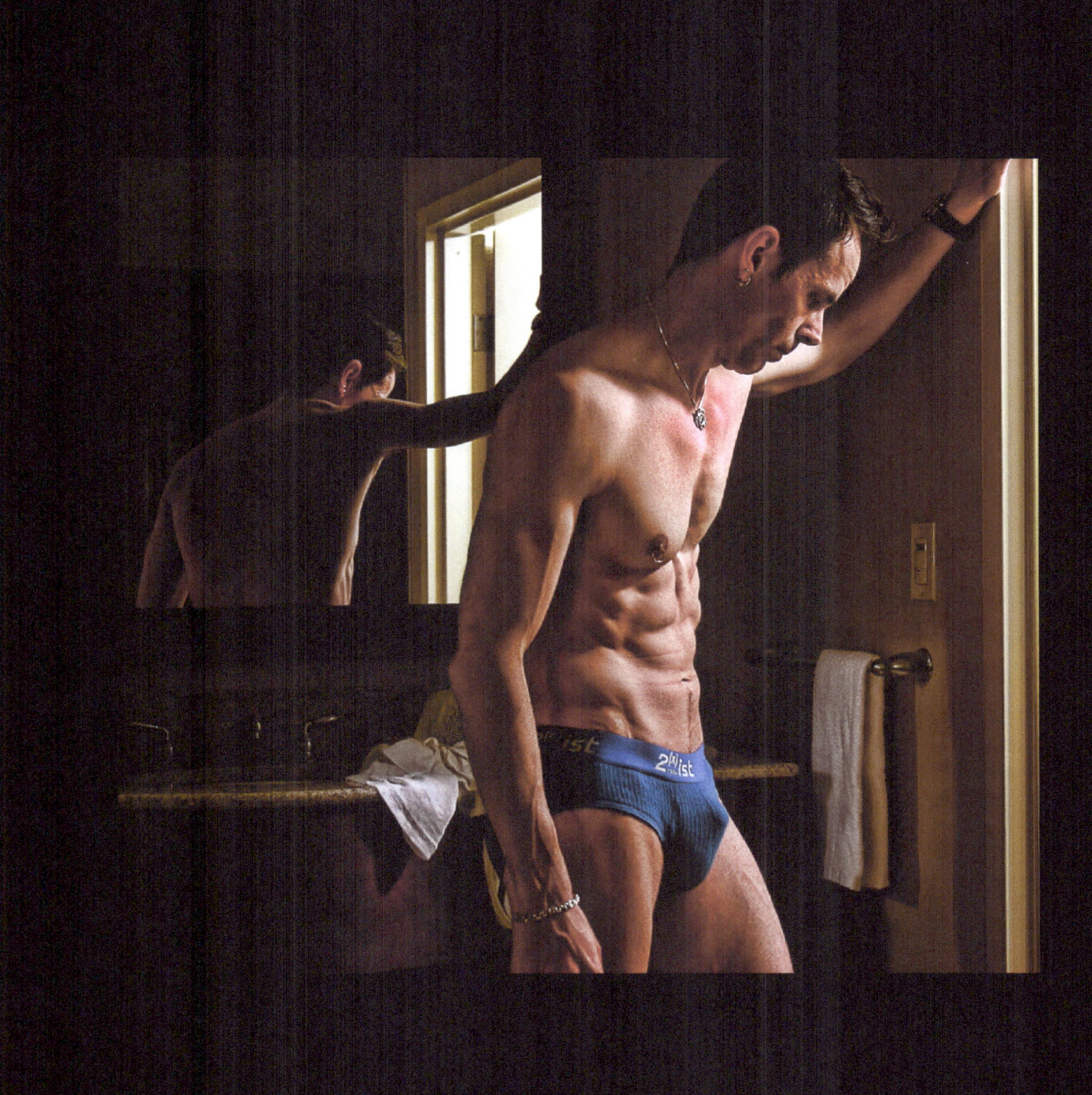

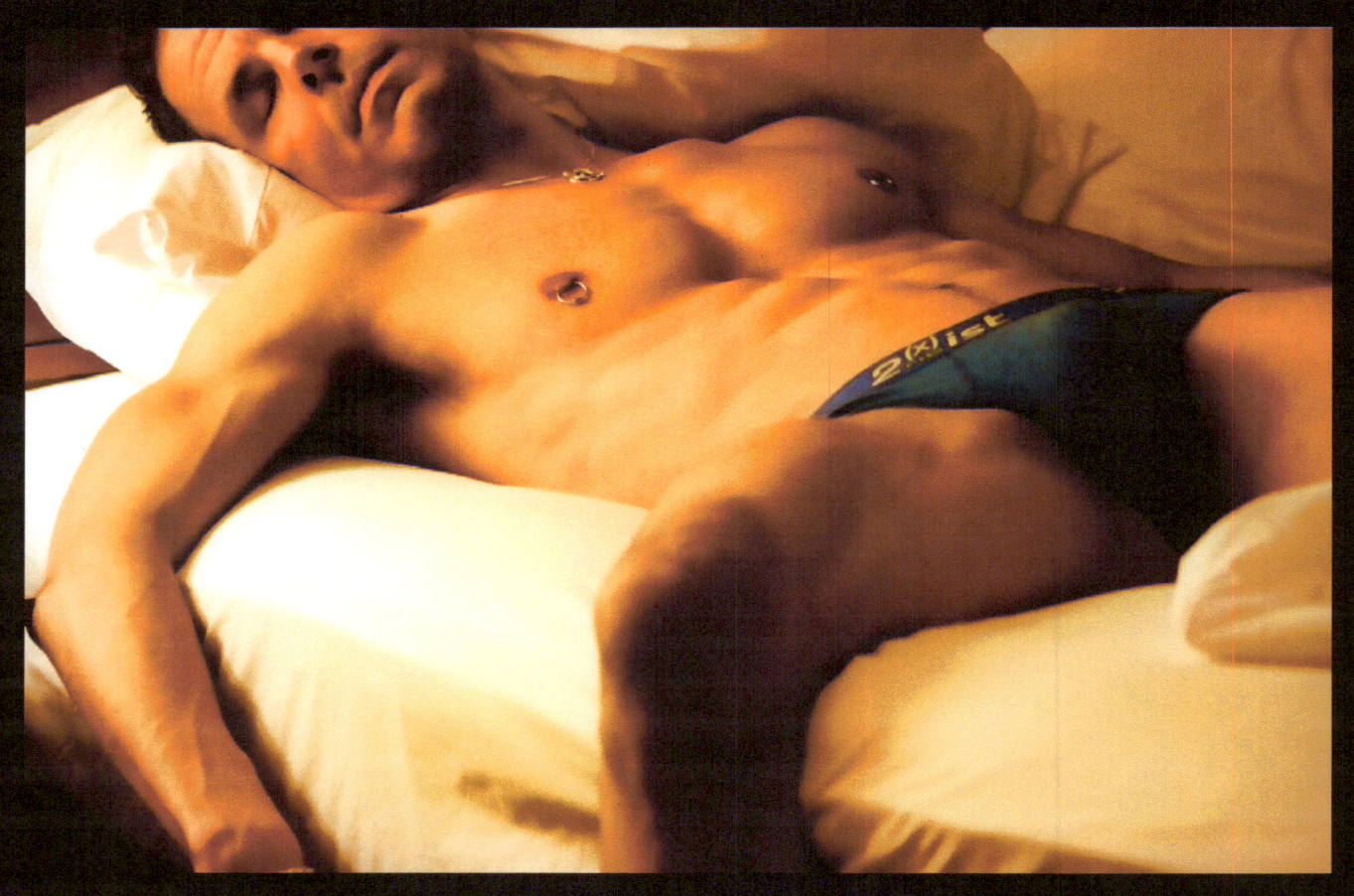

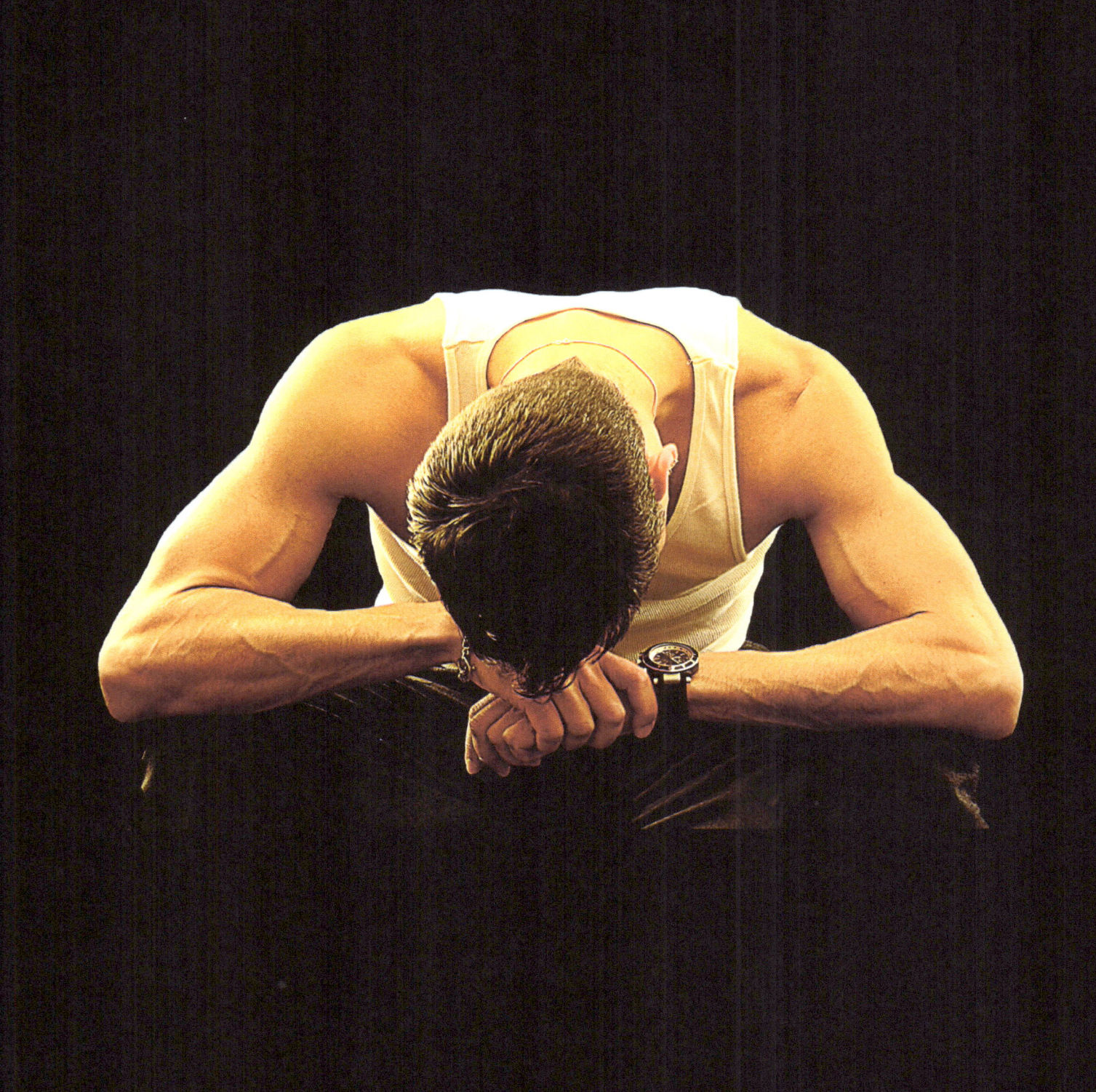

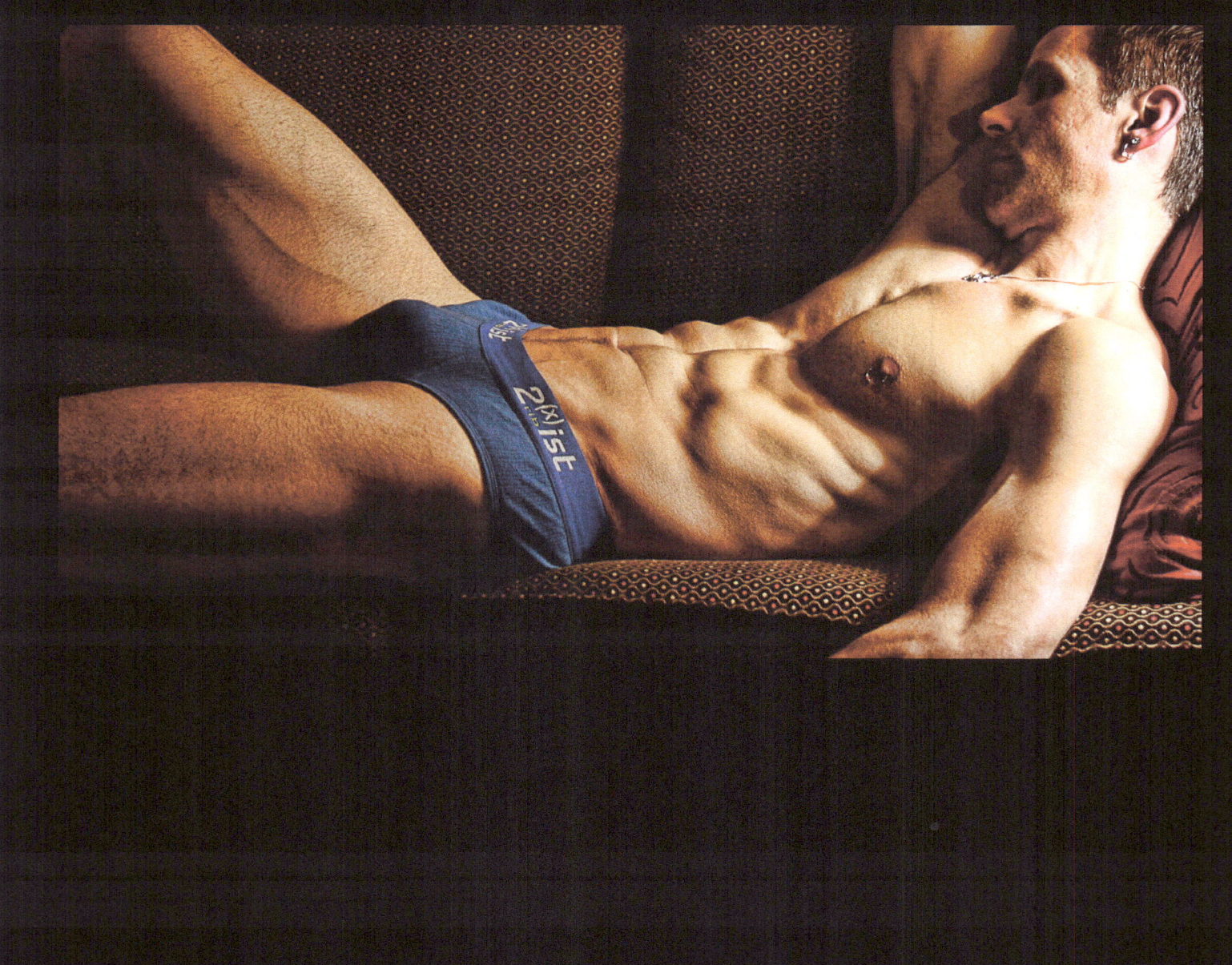

Jake

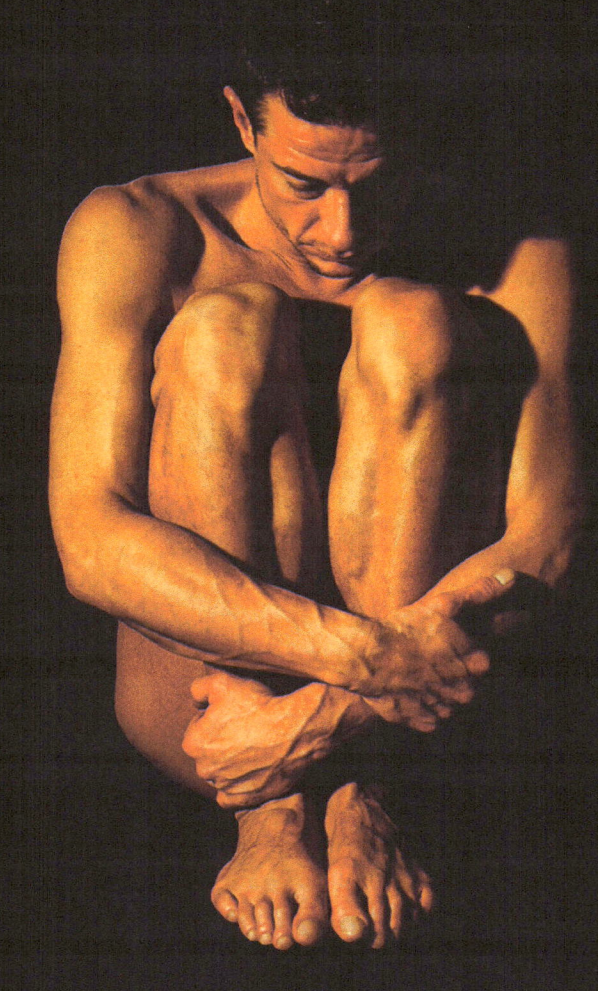

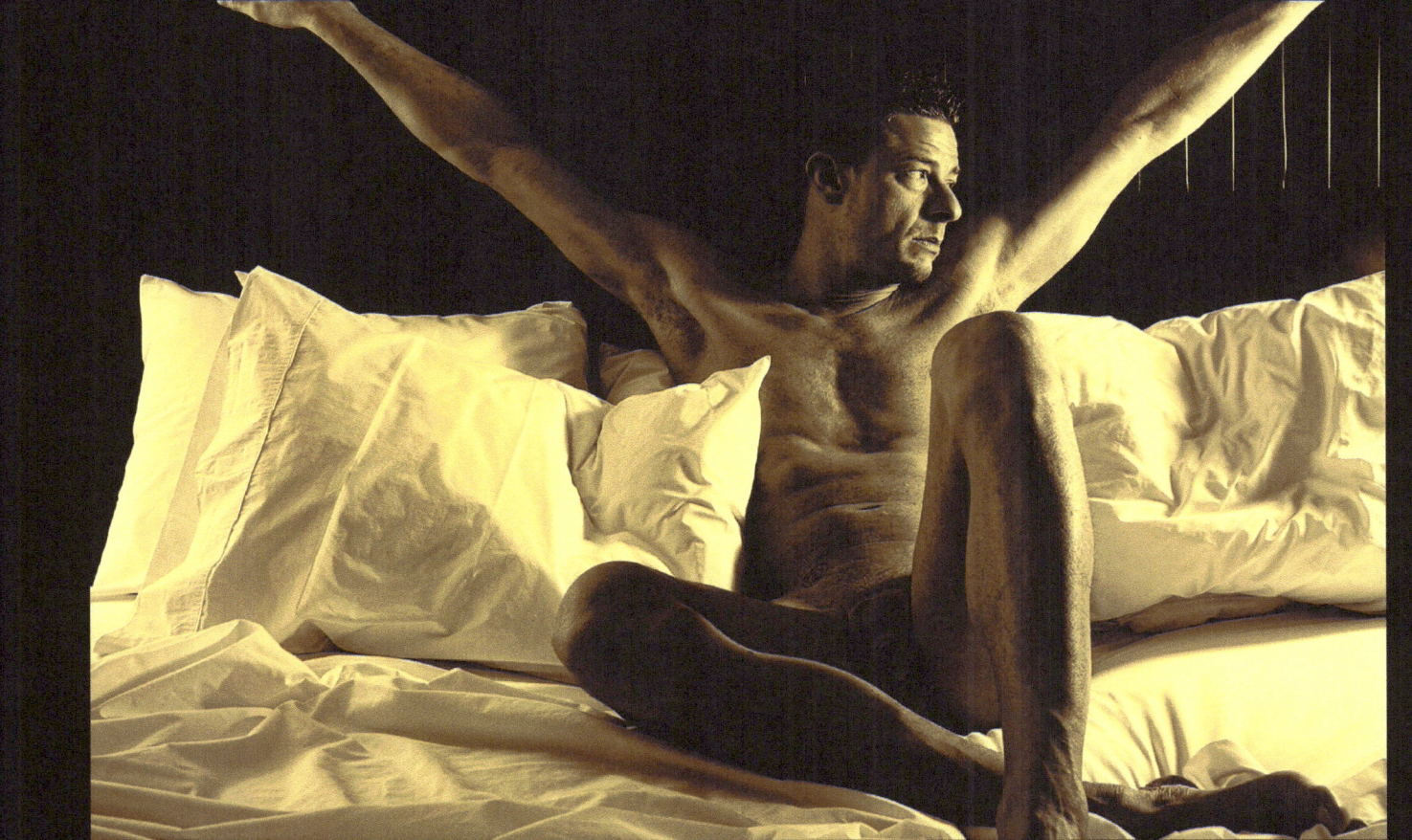

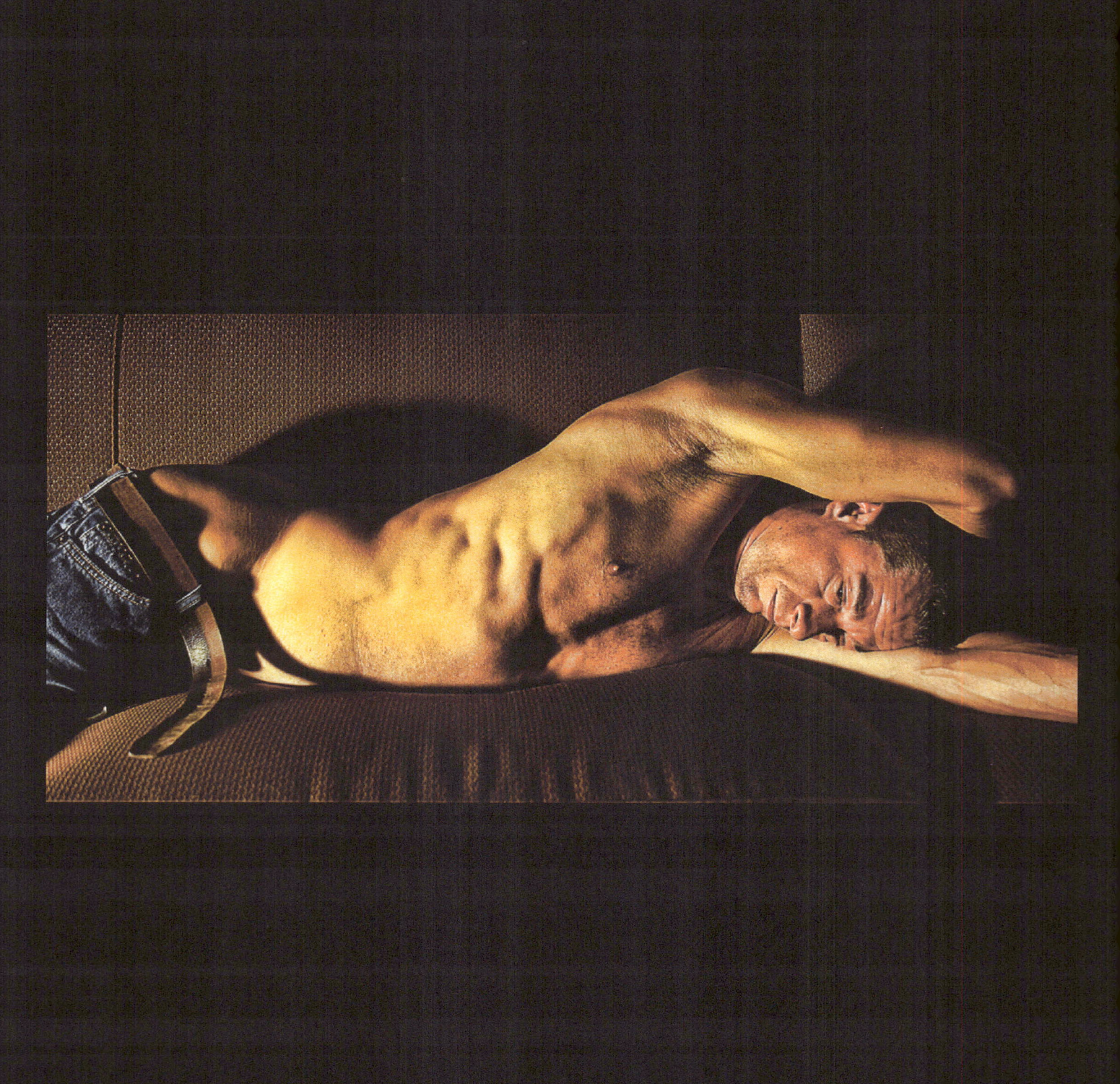

Anthony
(Marco)

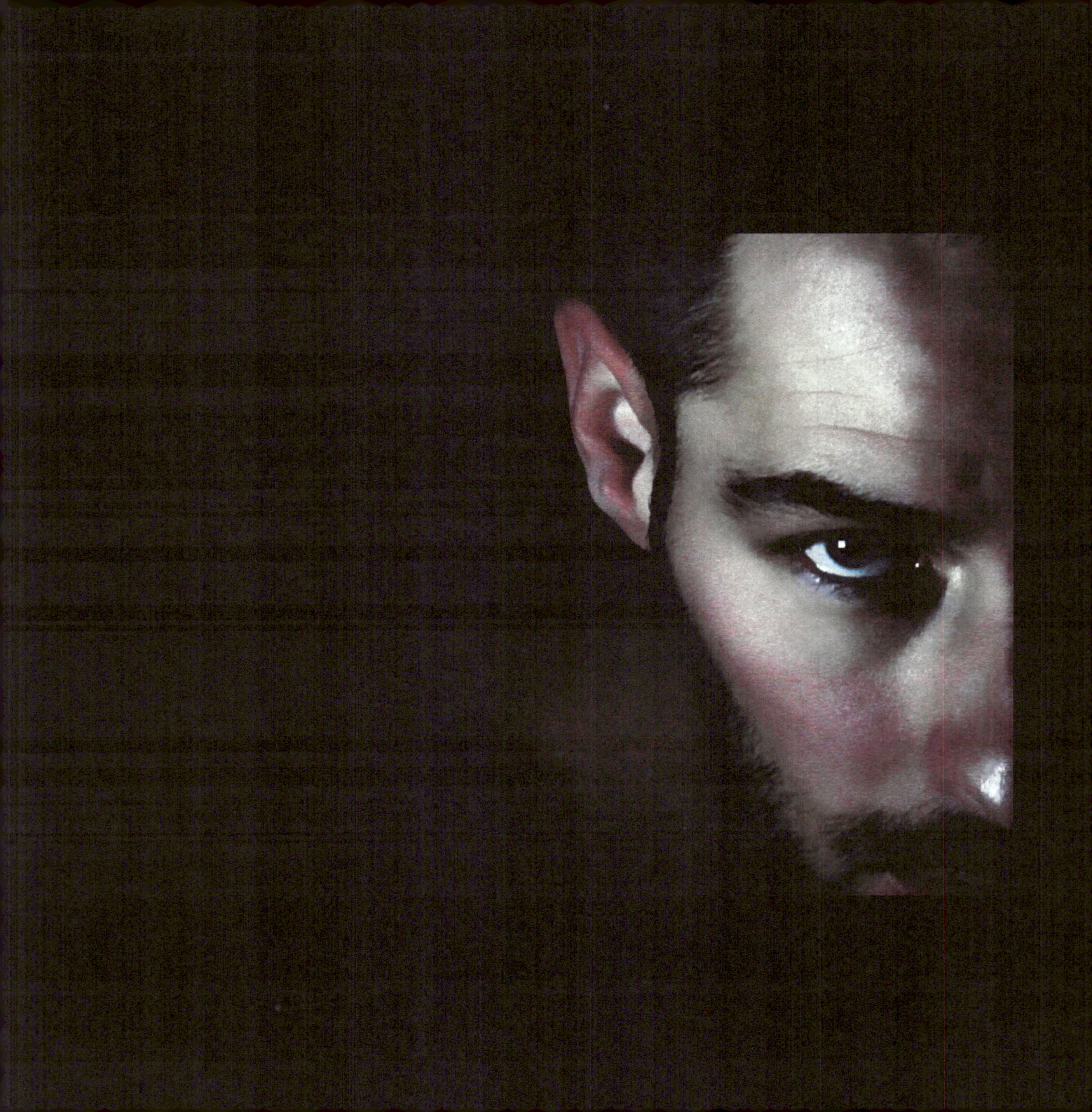

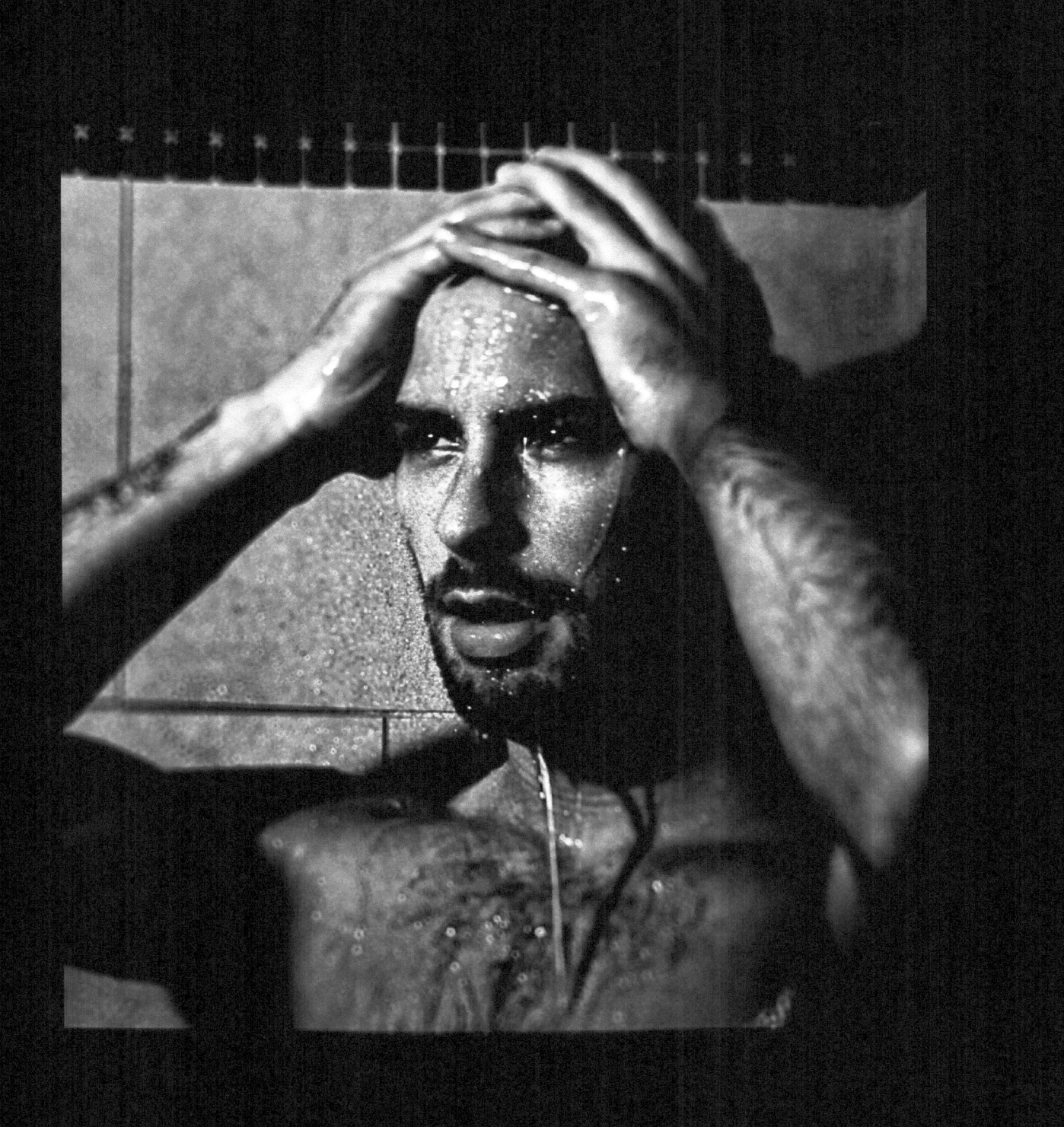

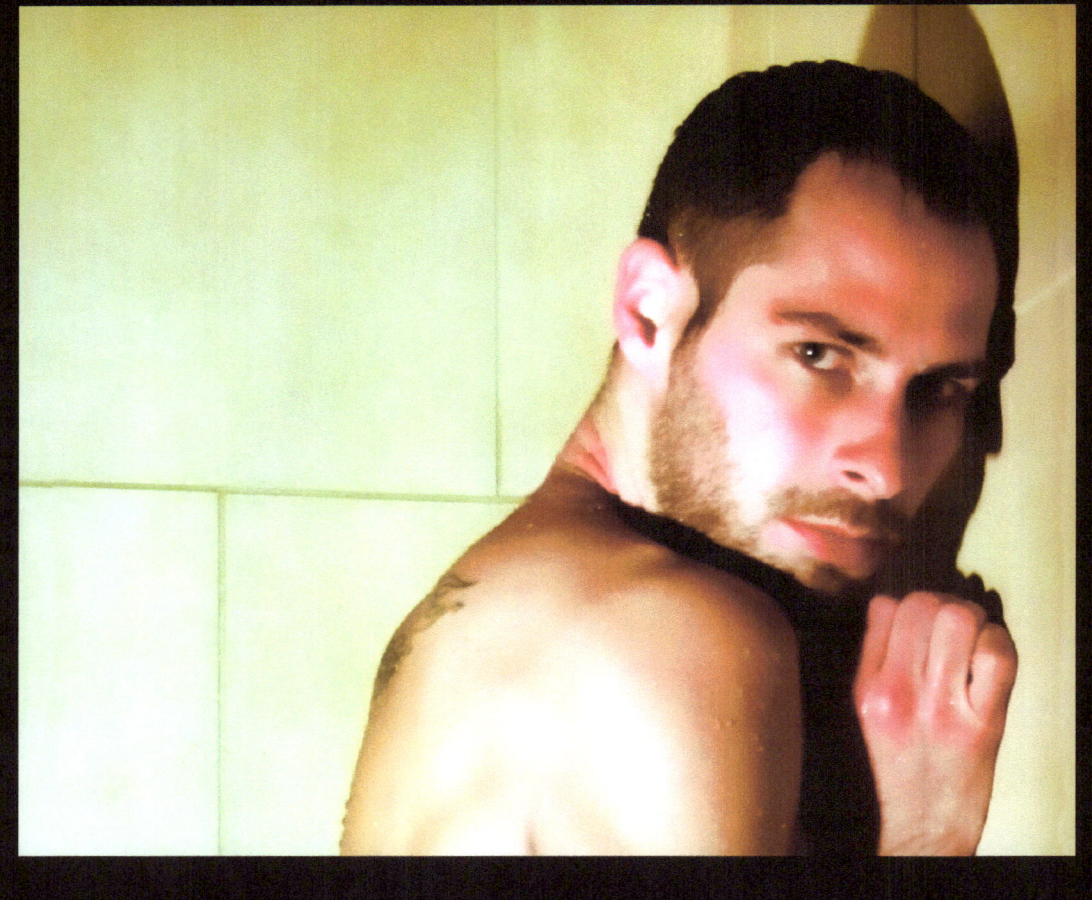

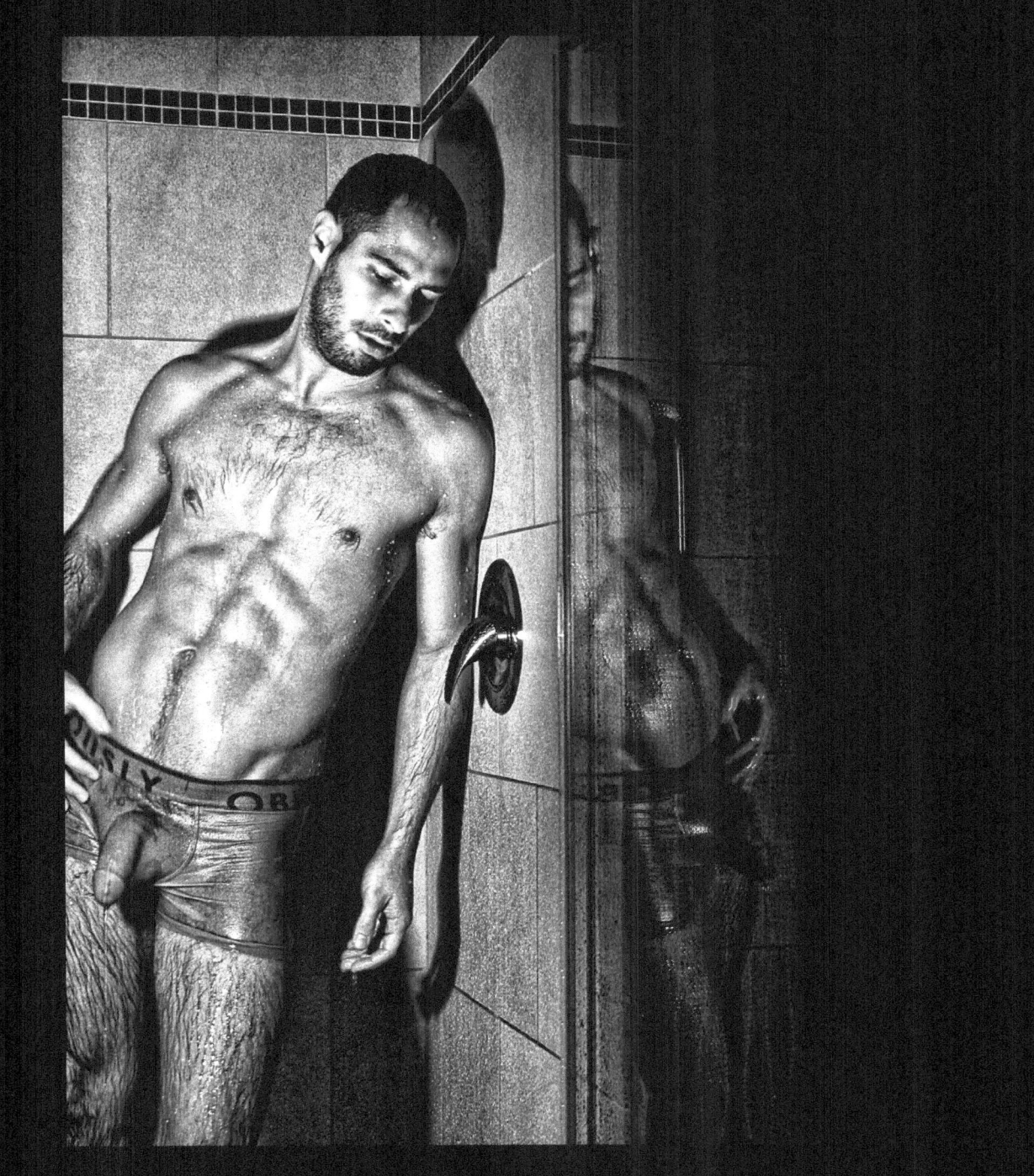

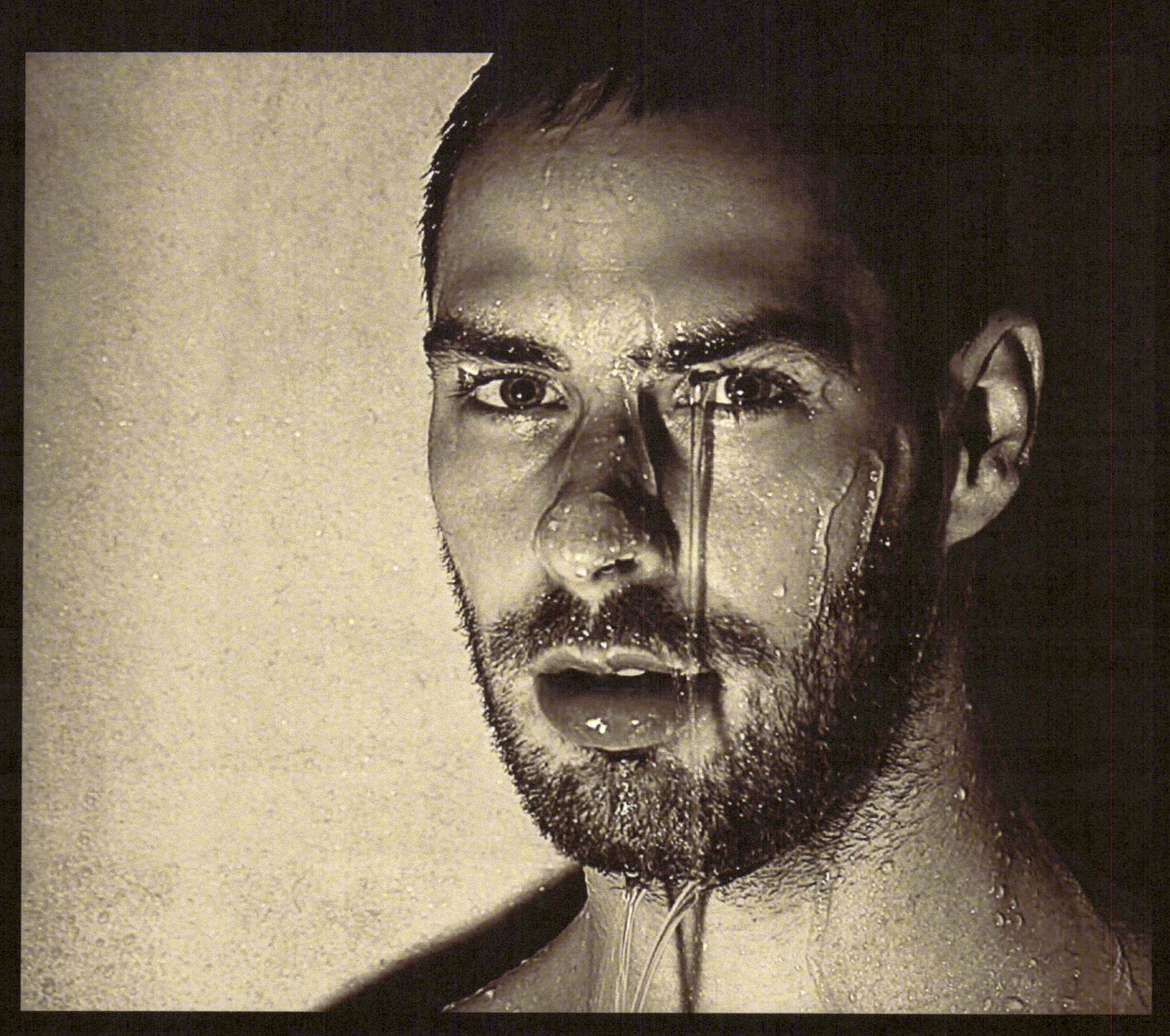

Jake
&
Marco

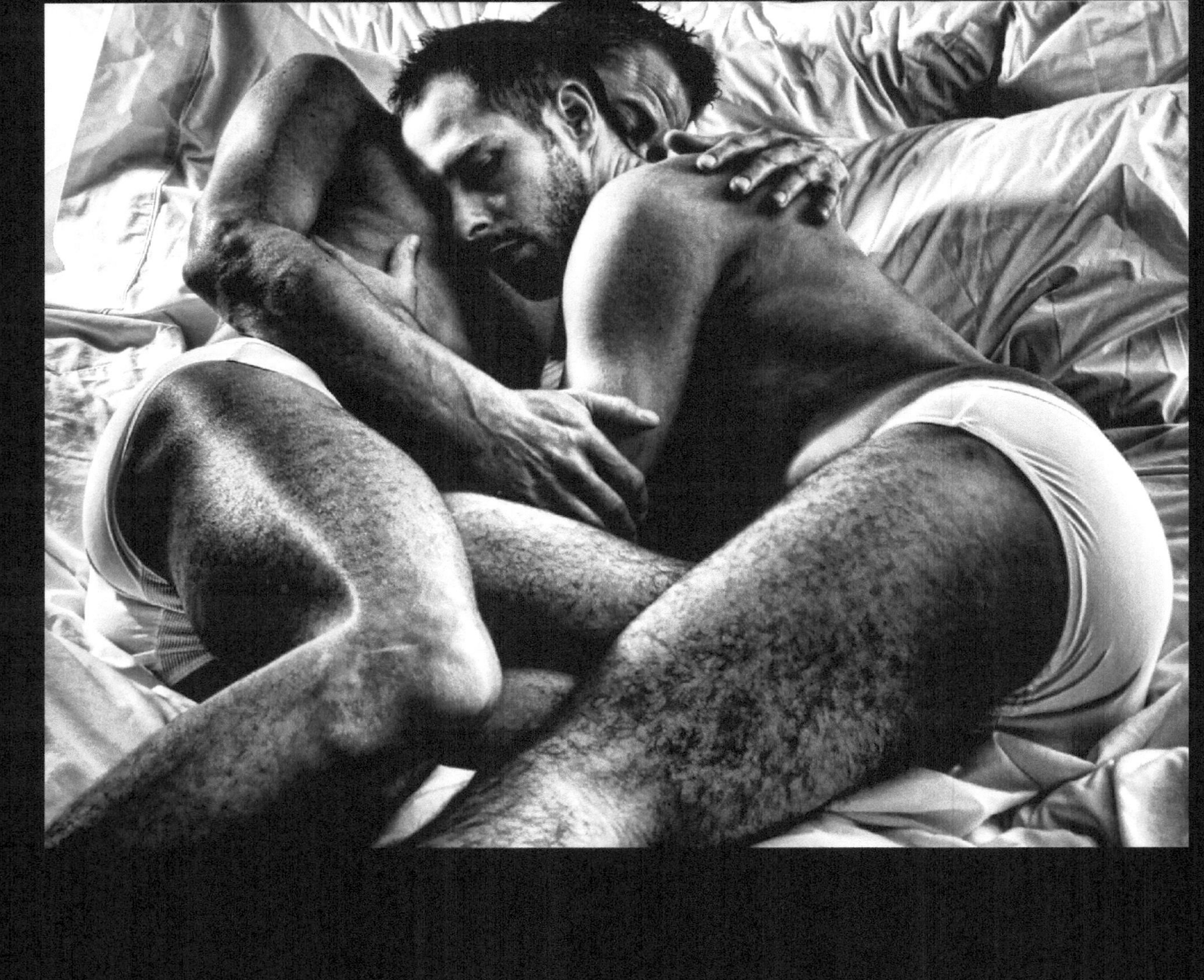

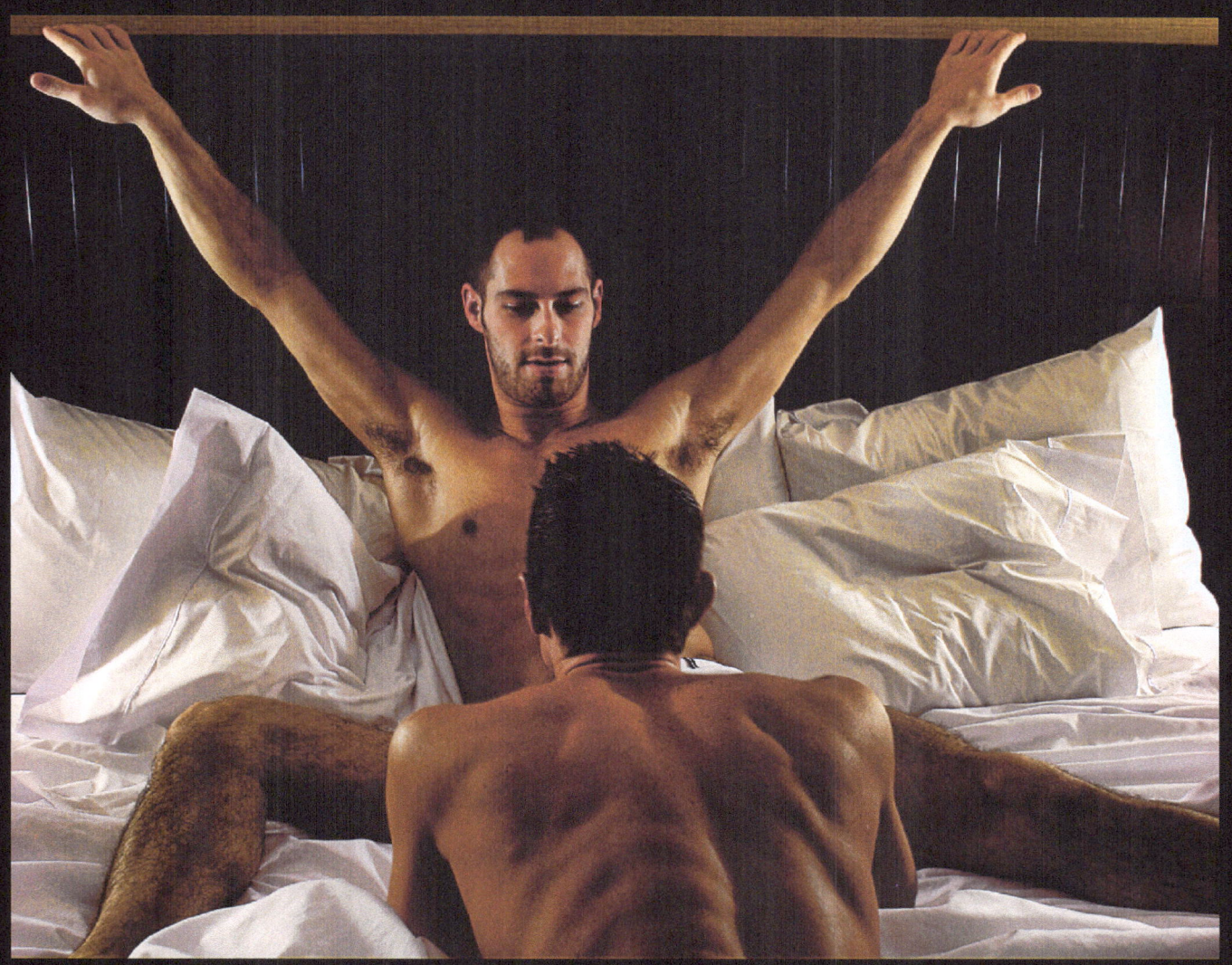

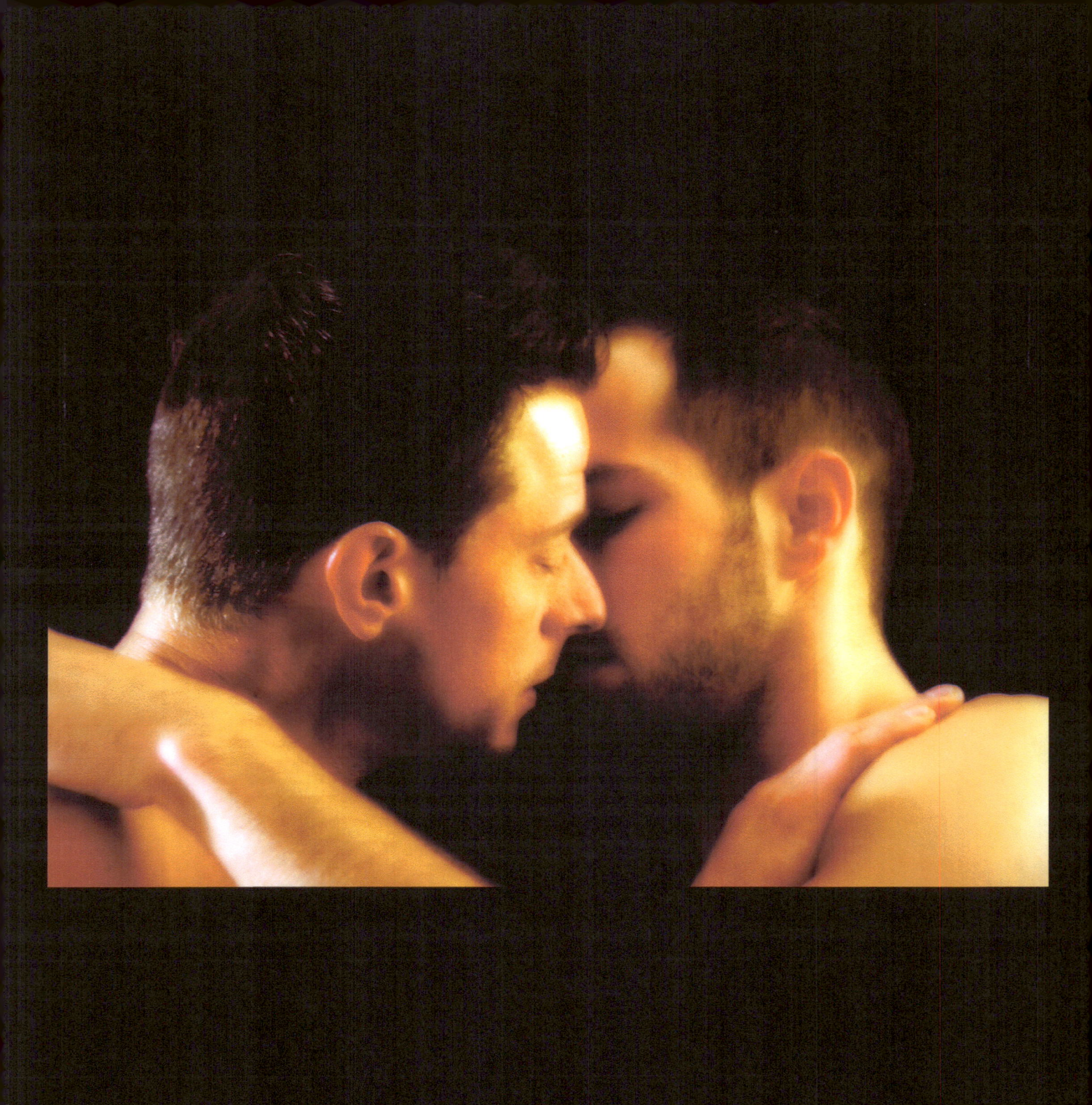

Michael

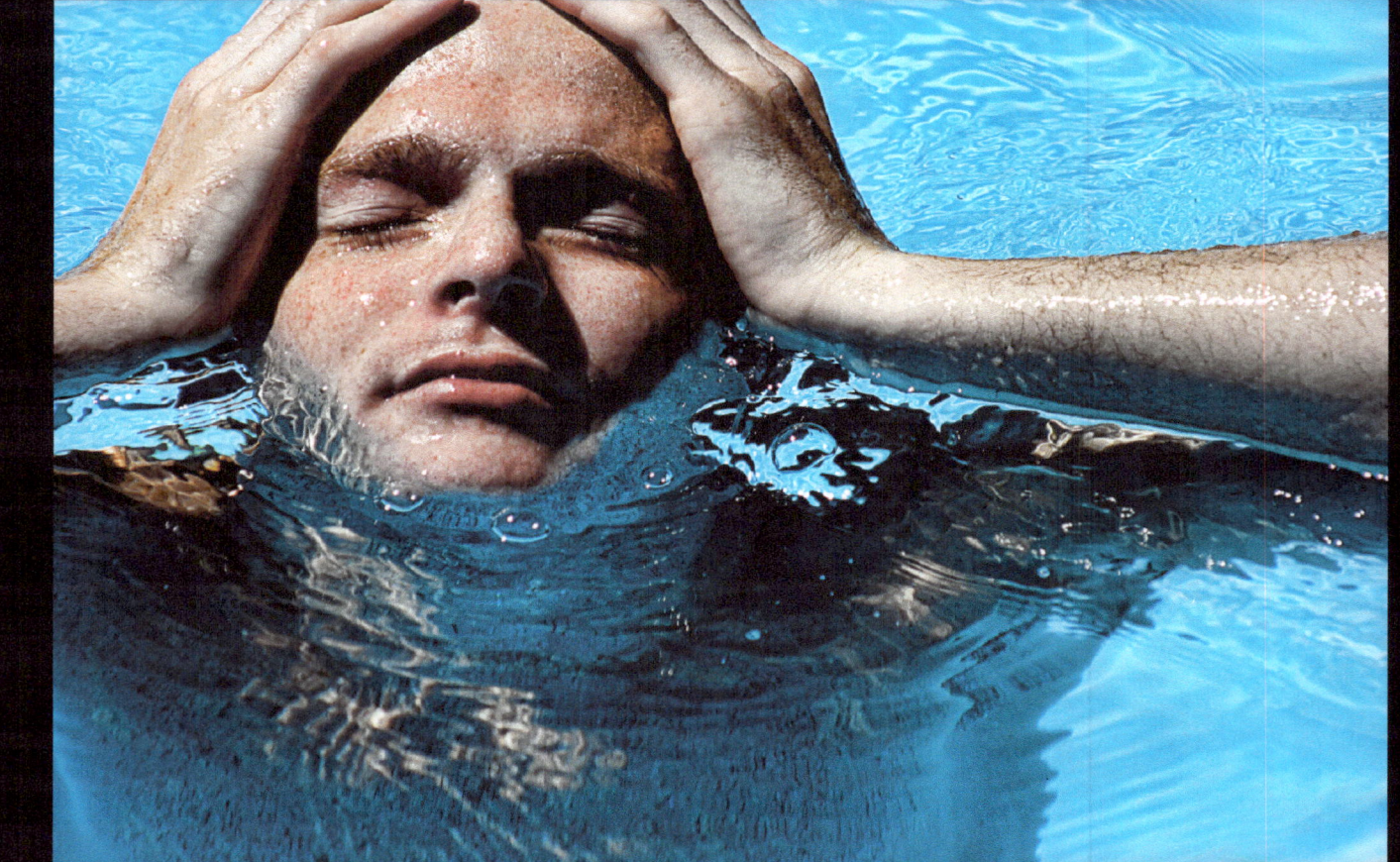

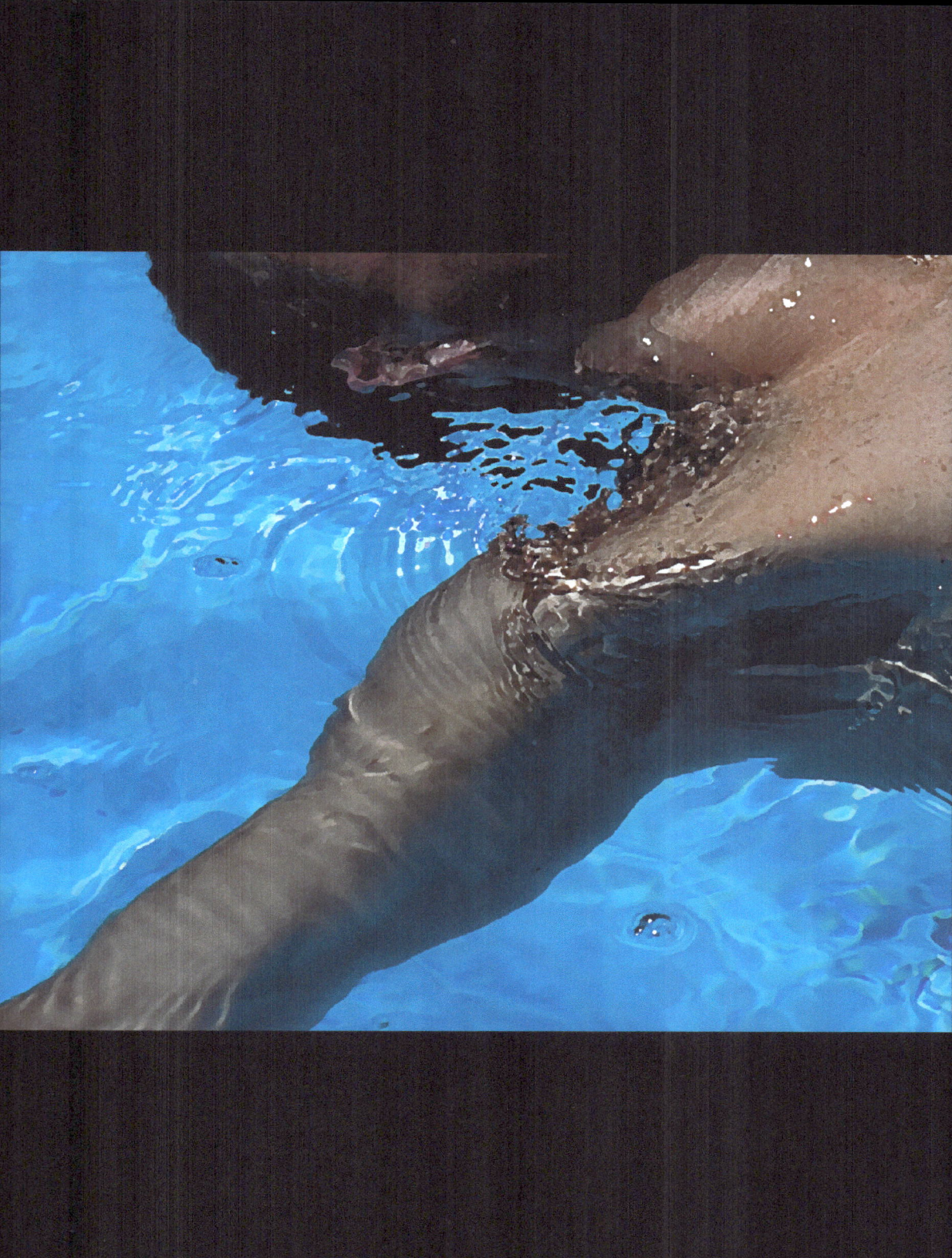

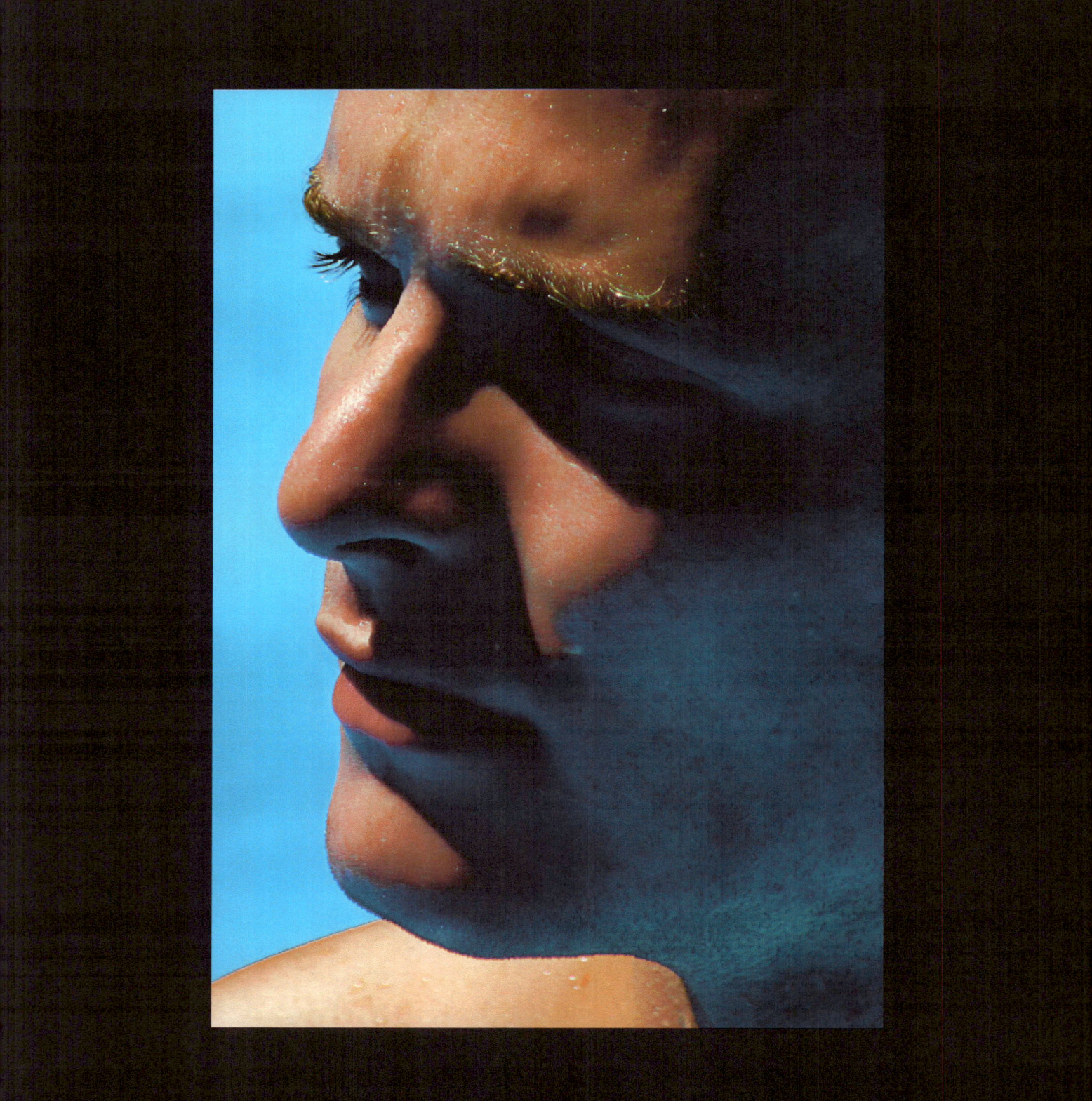

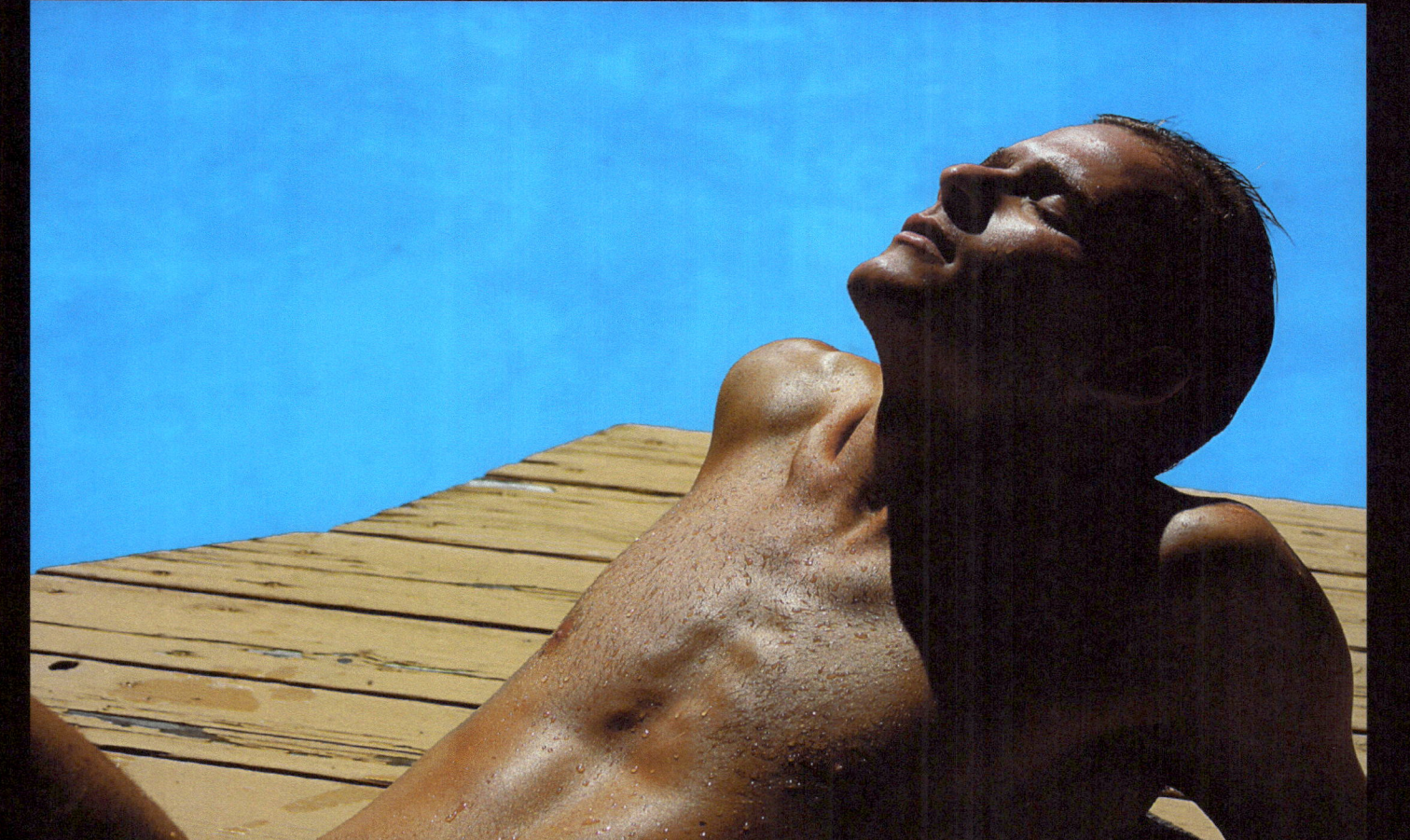

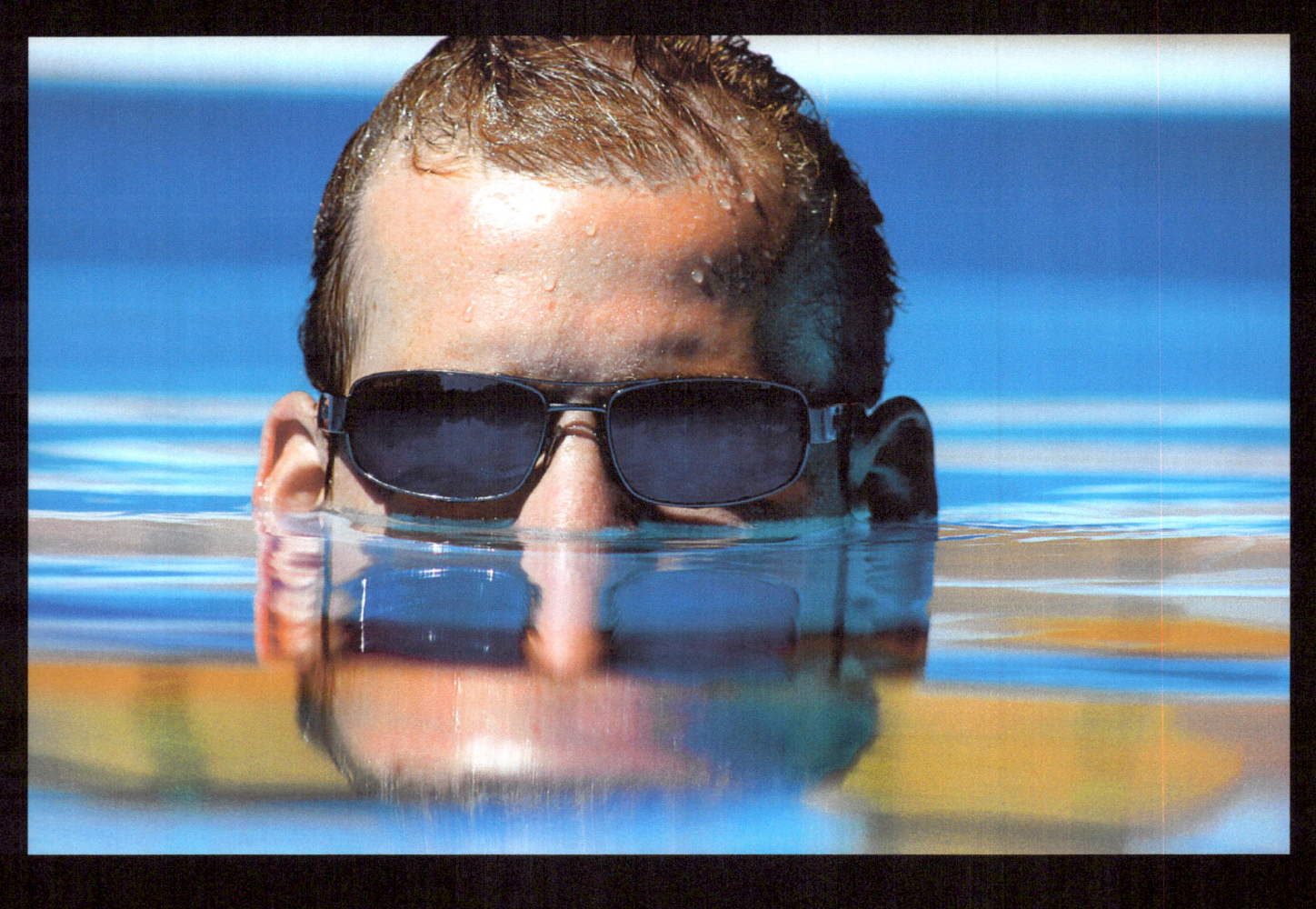

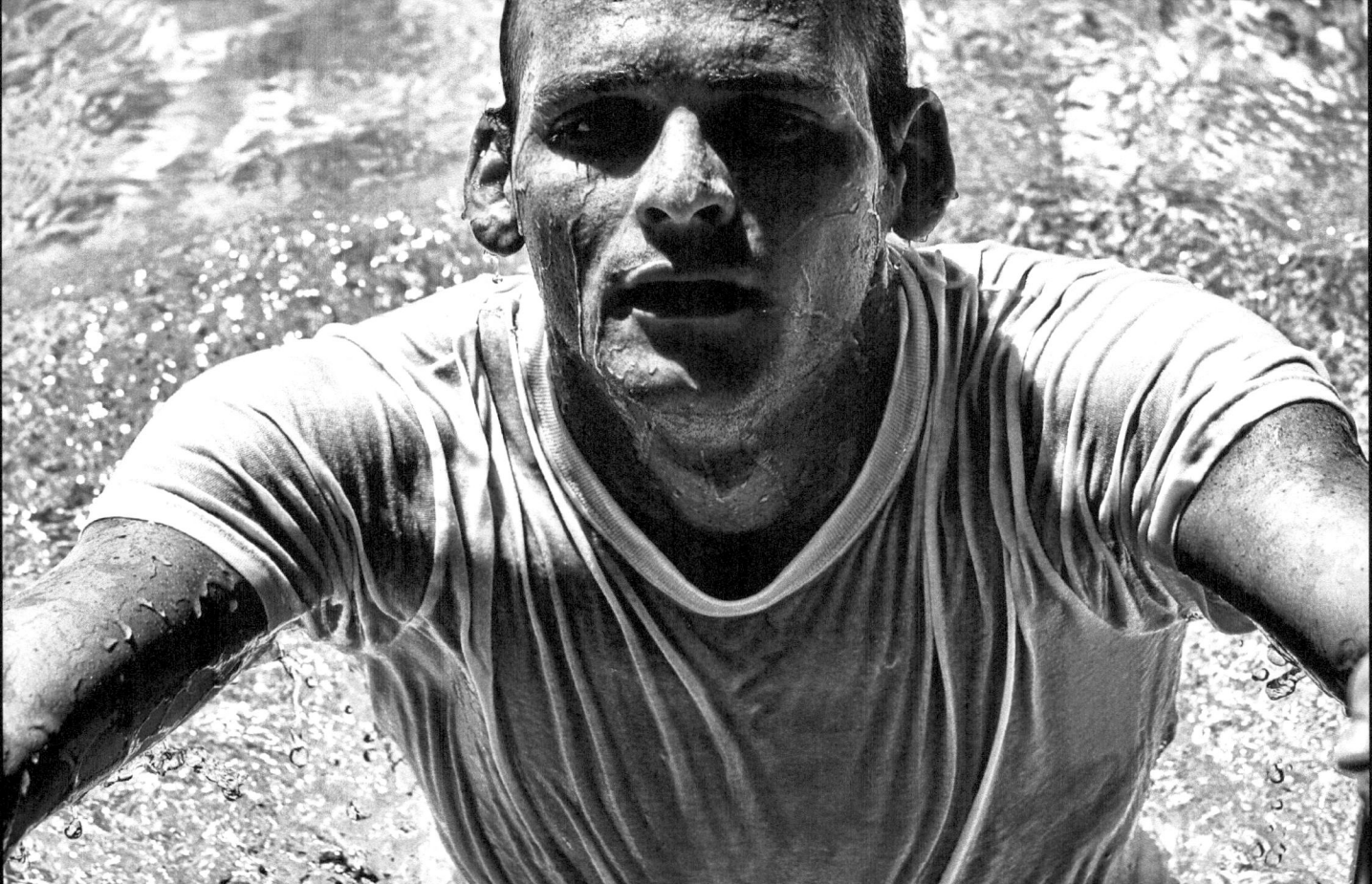

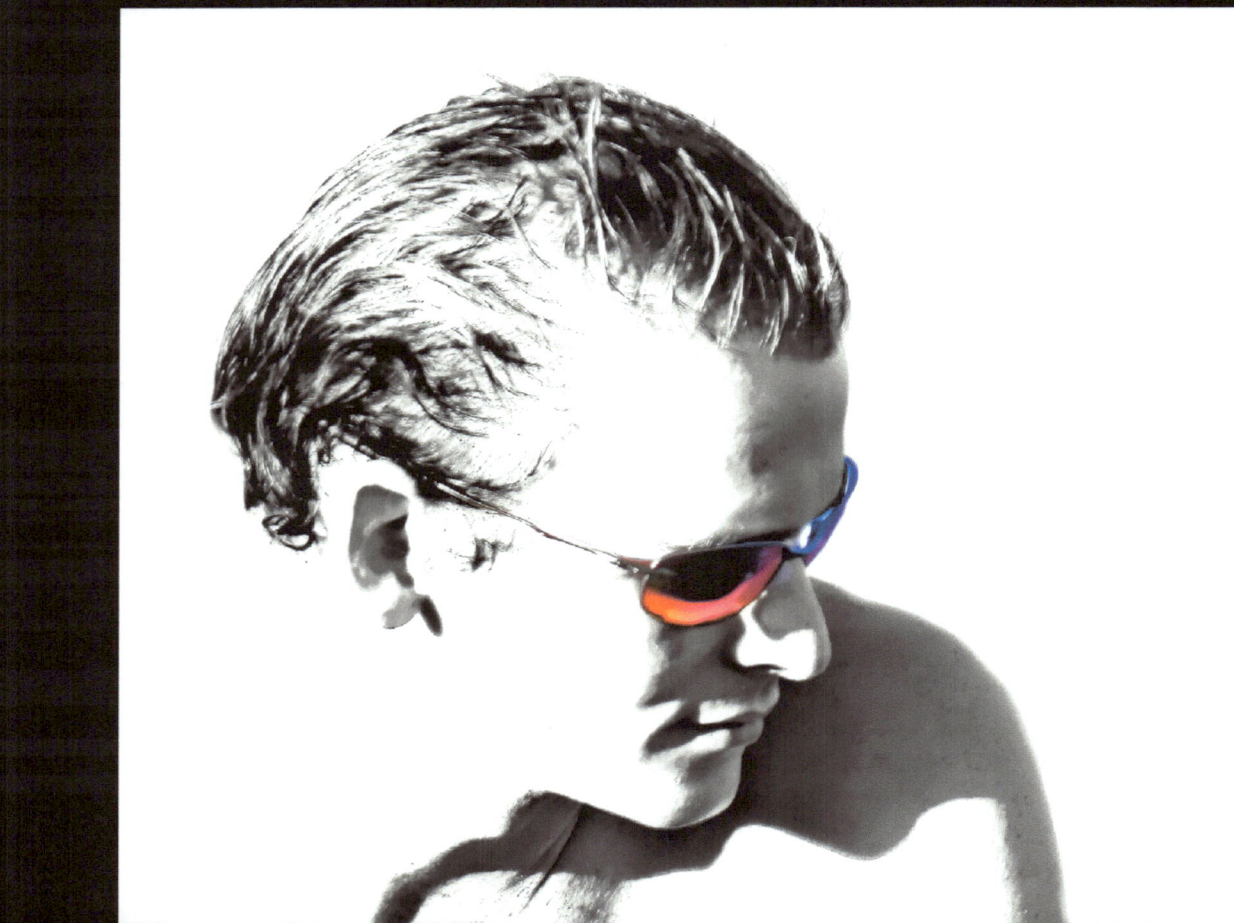

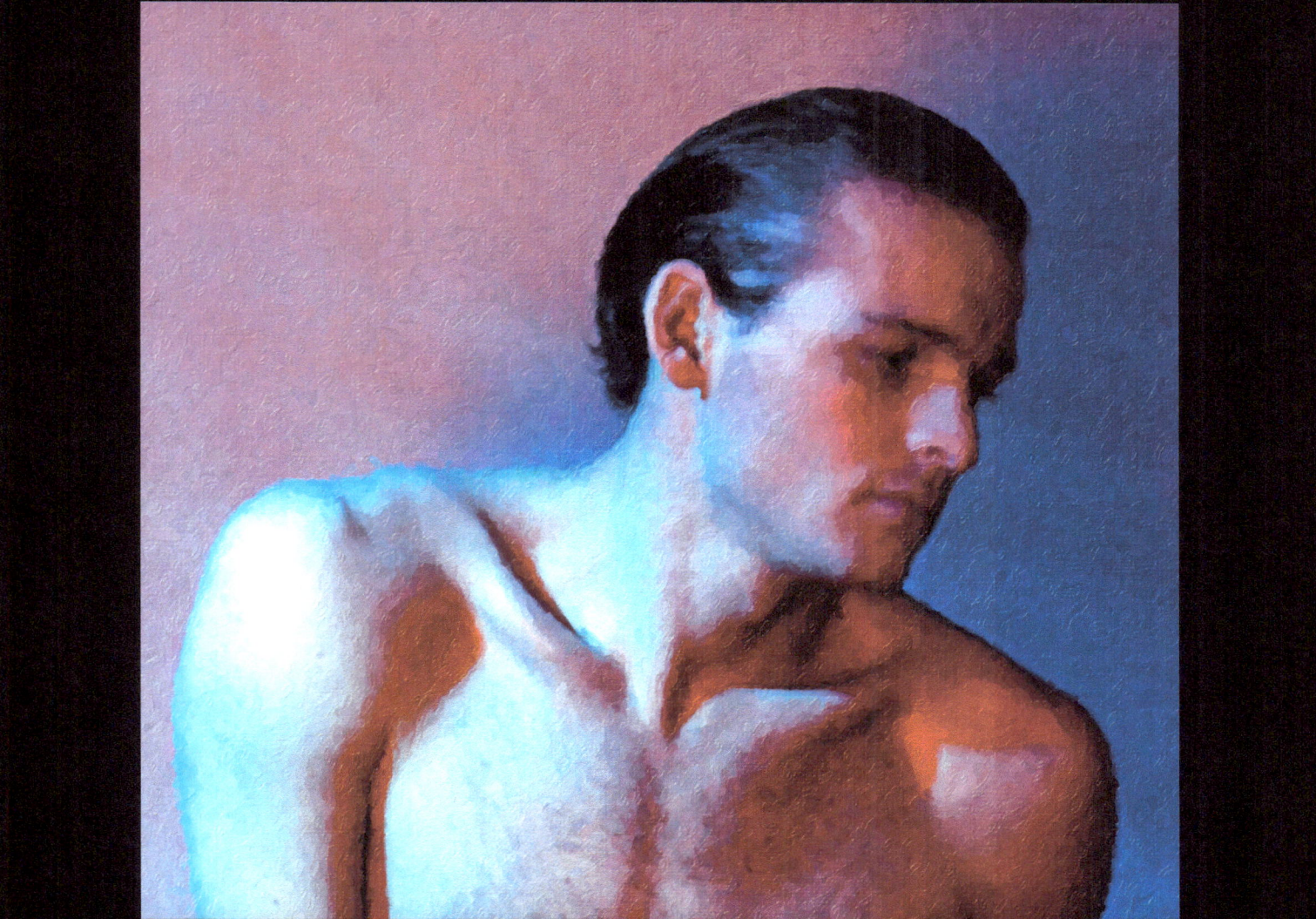

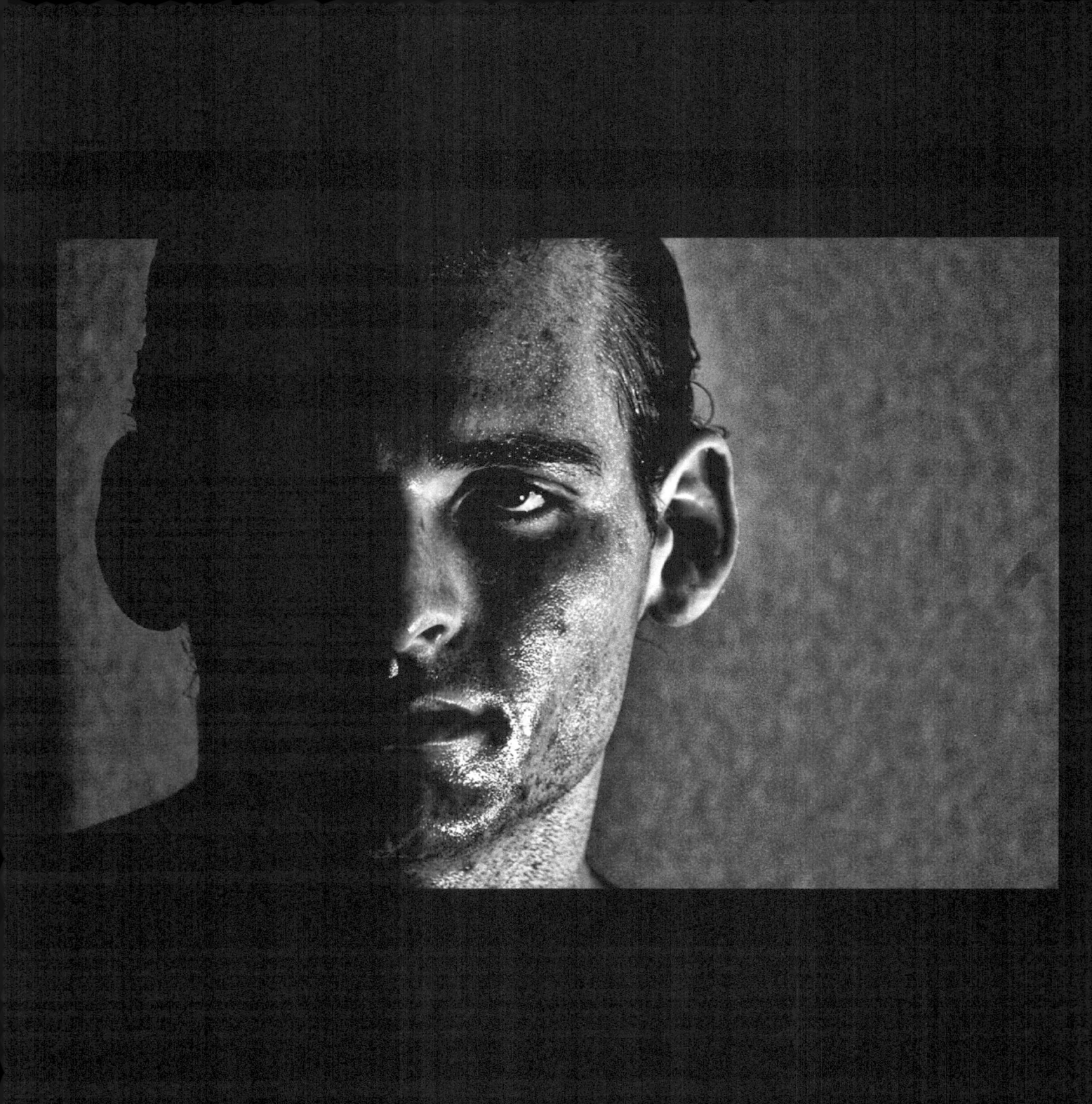

Patrick

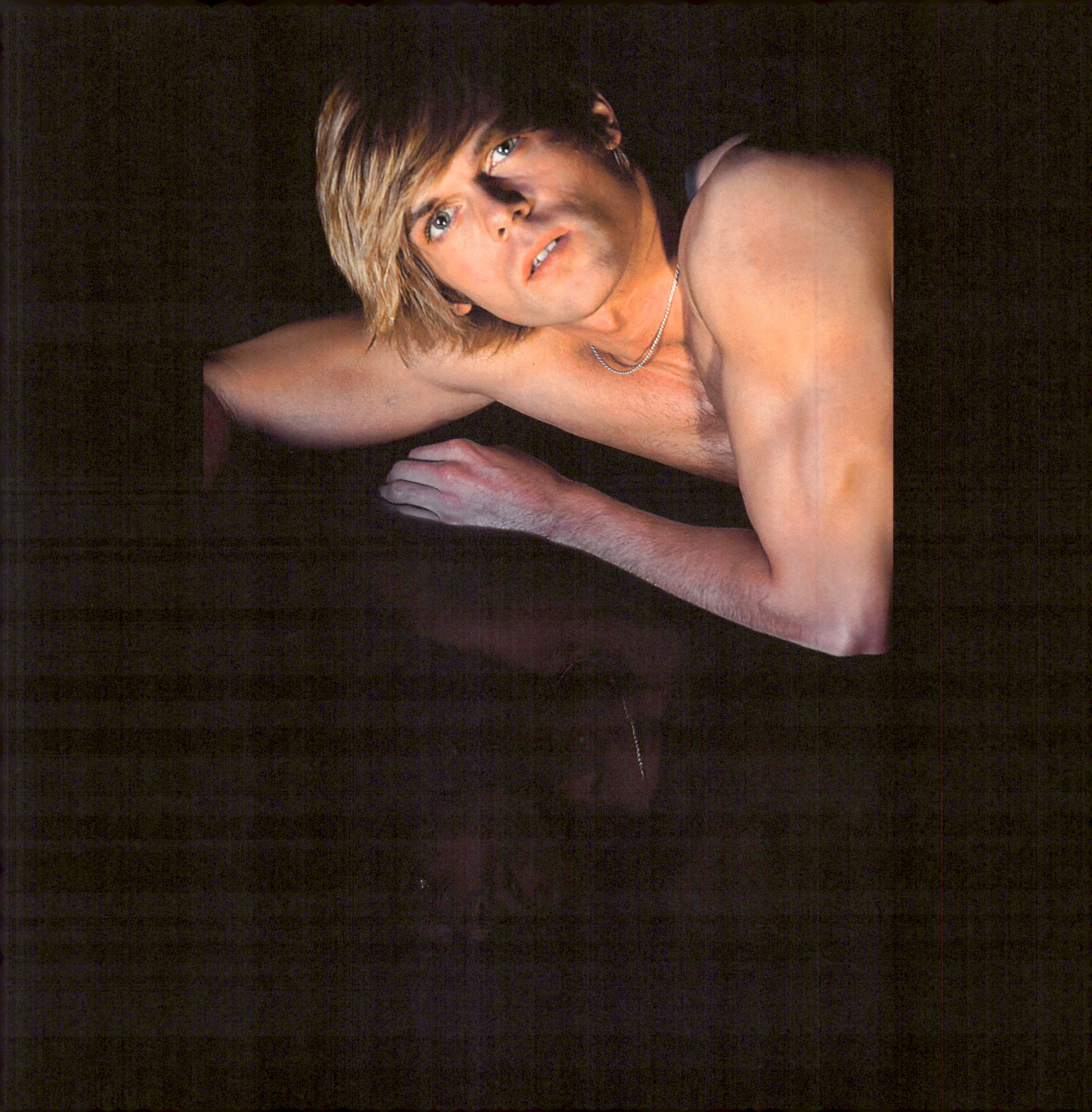

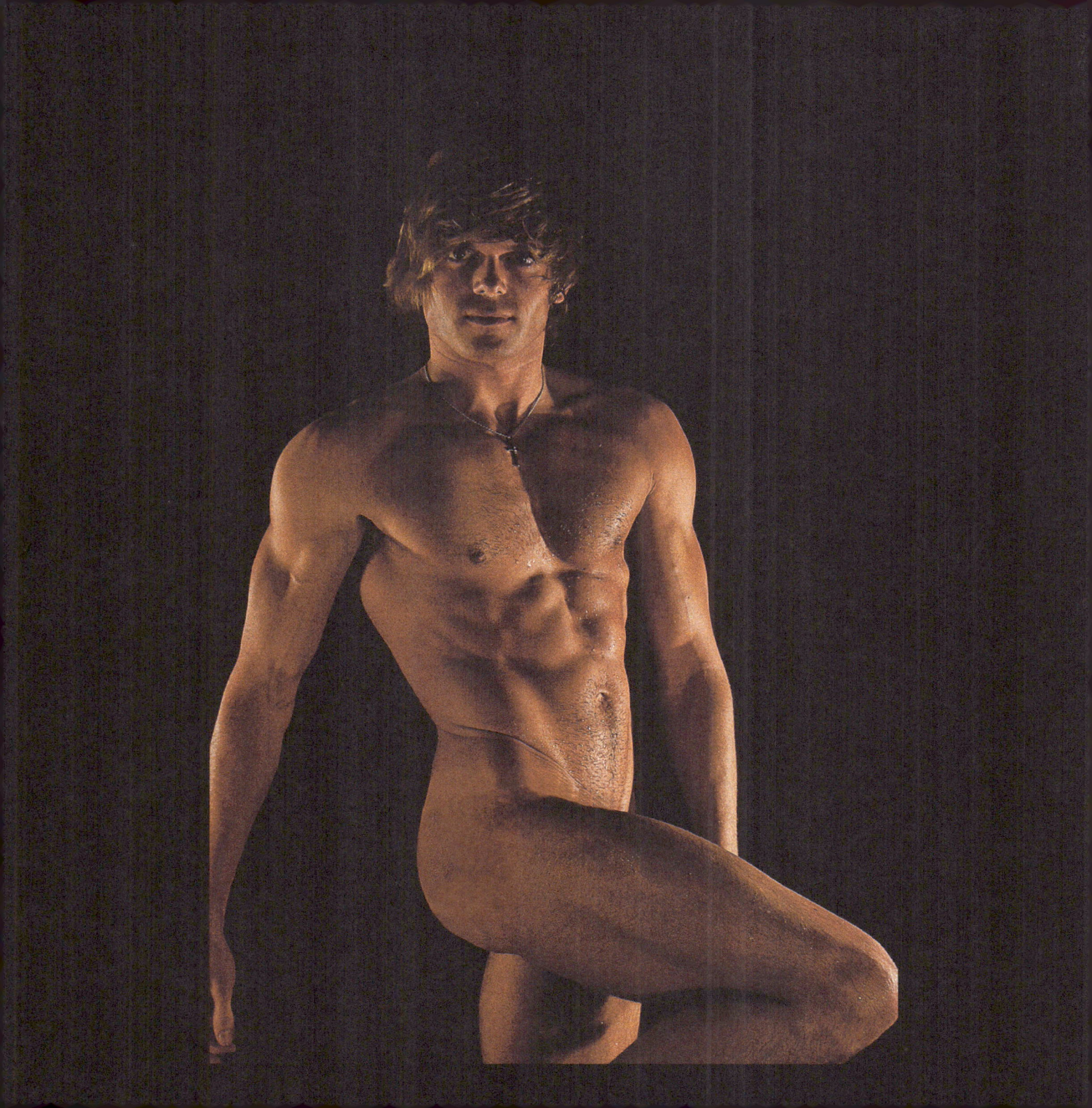

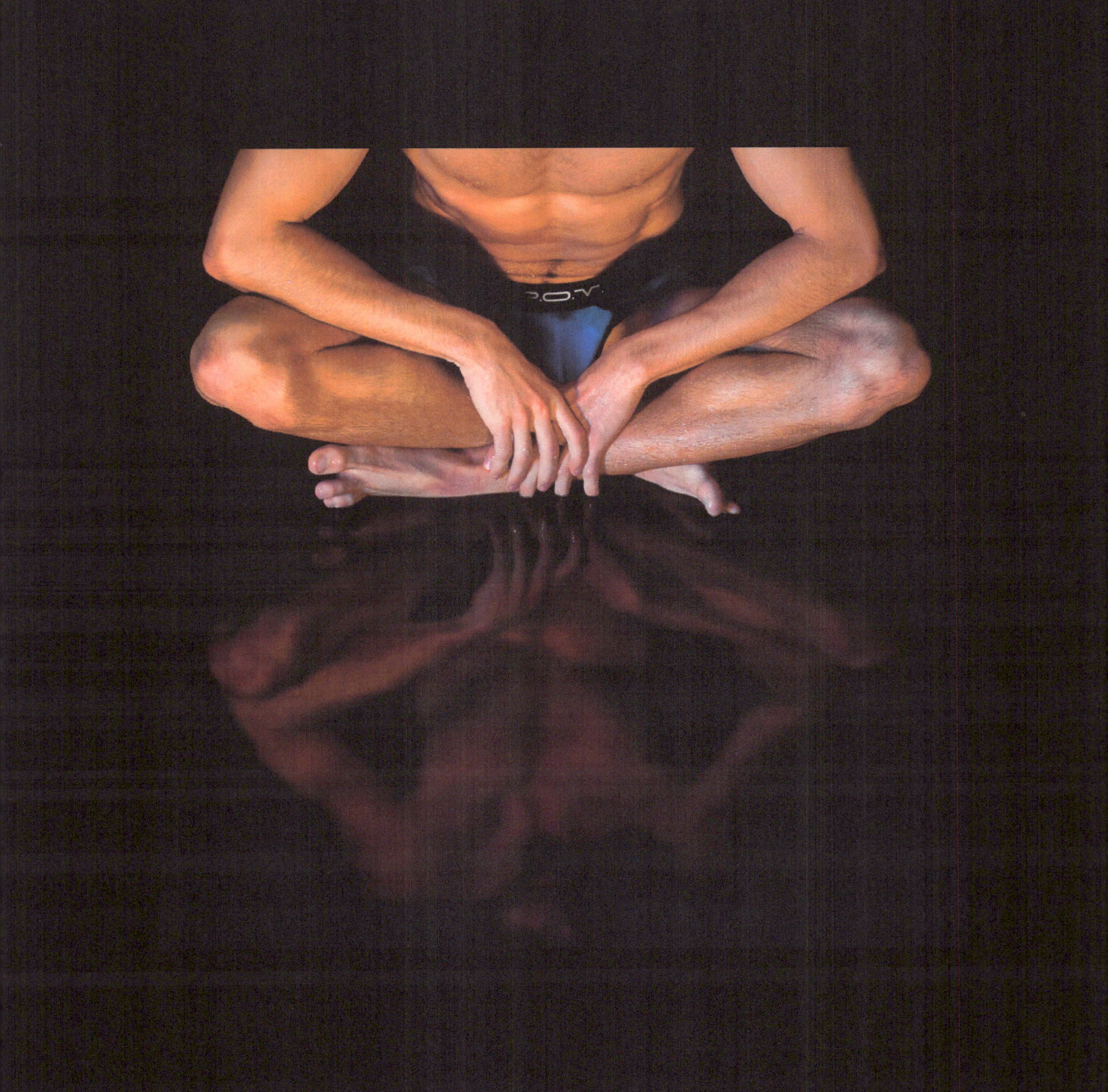

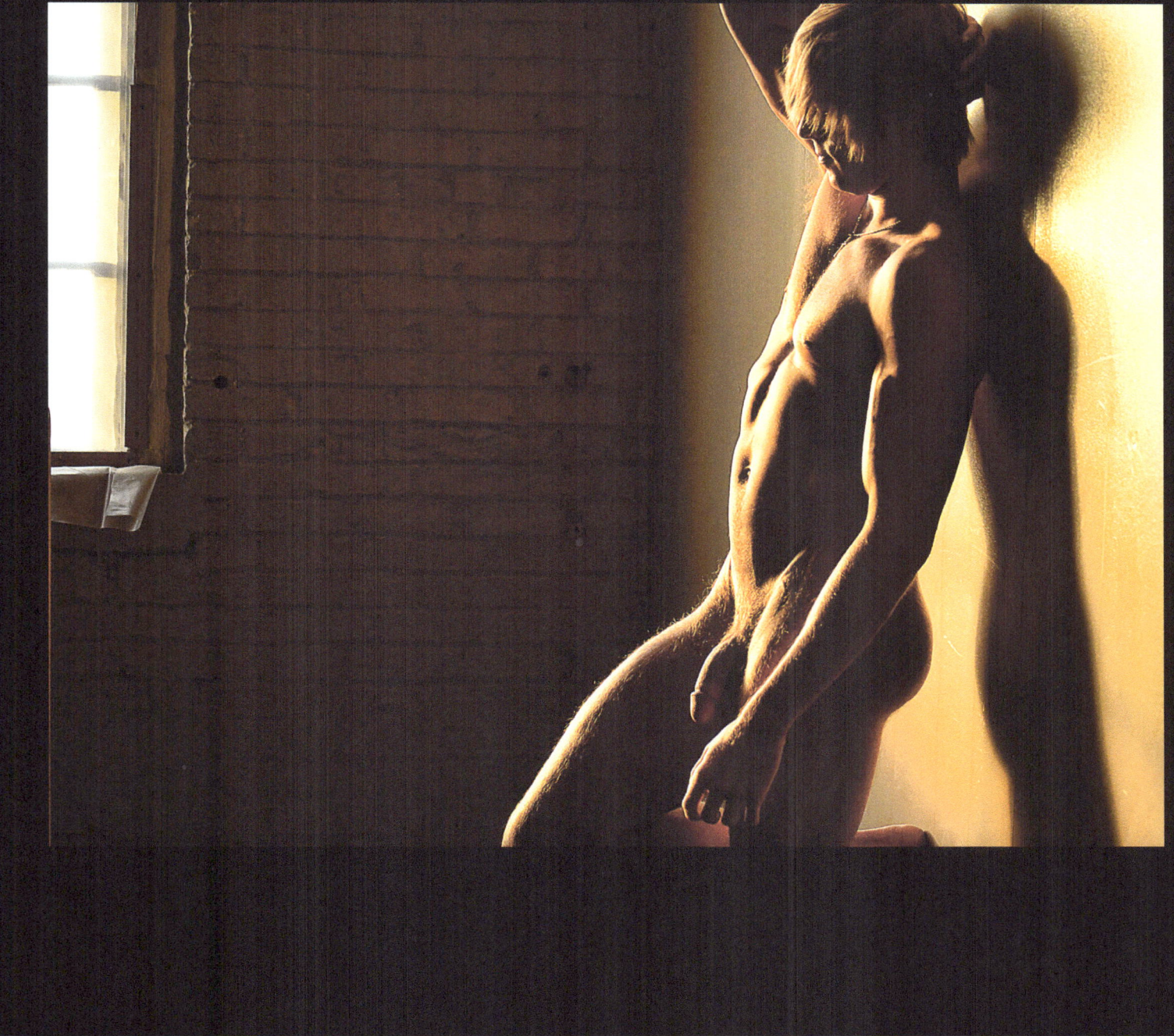

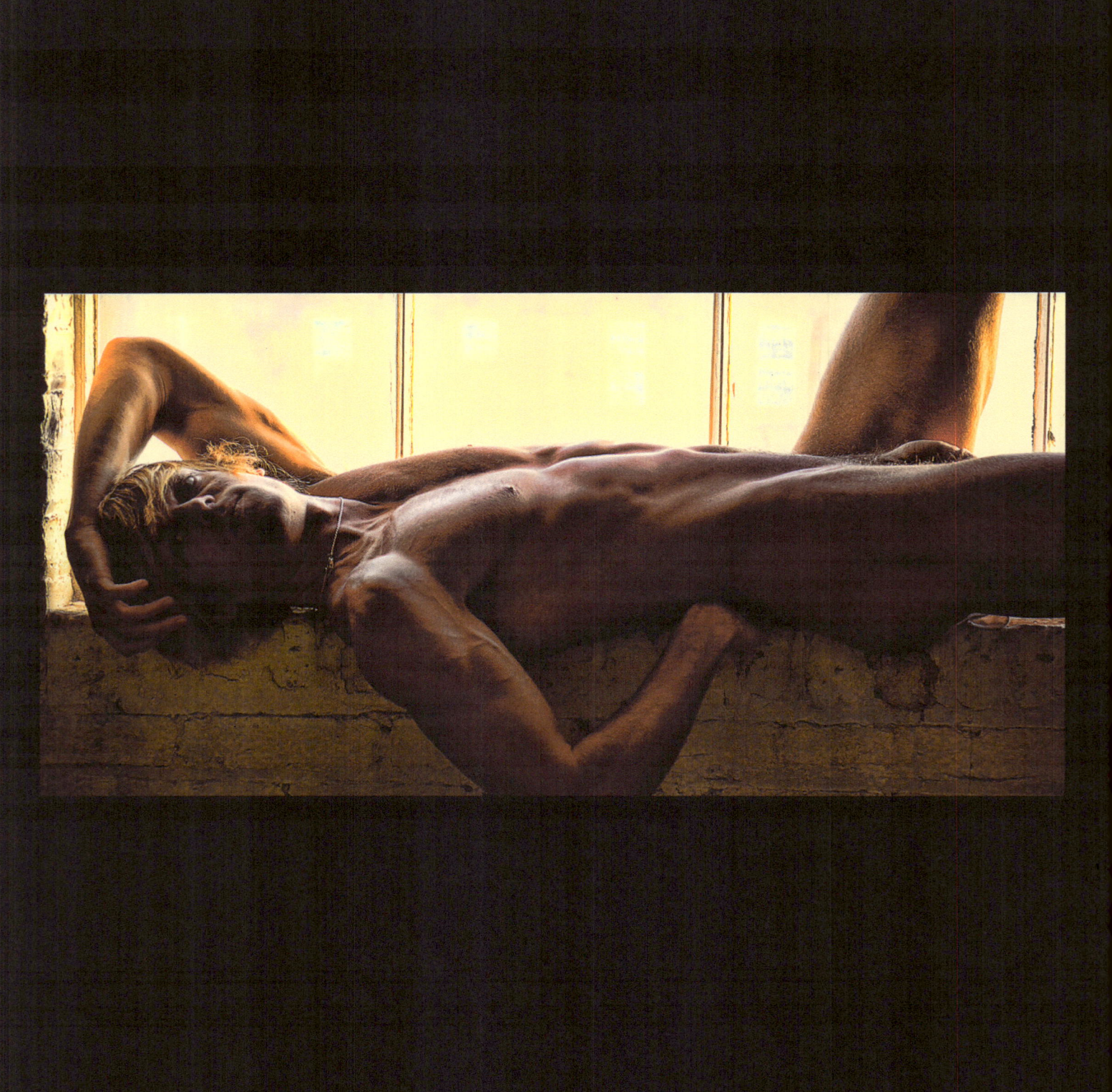

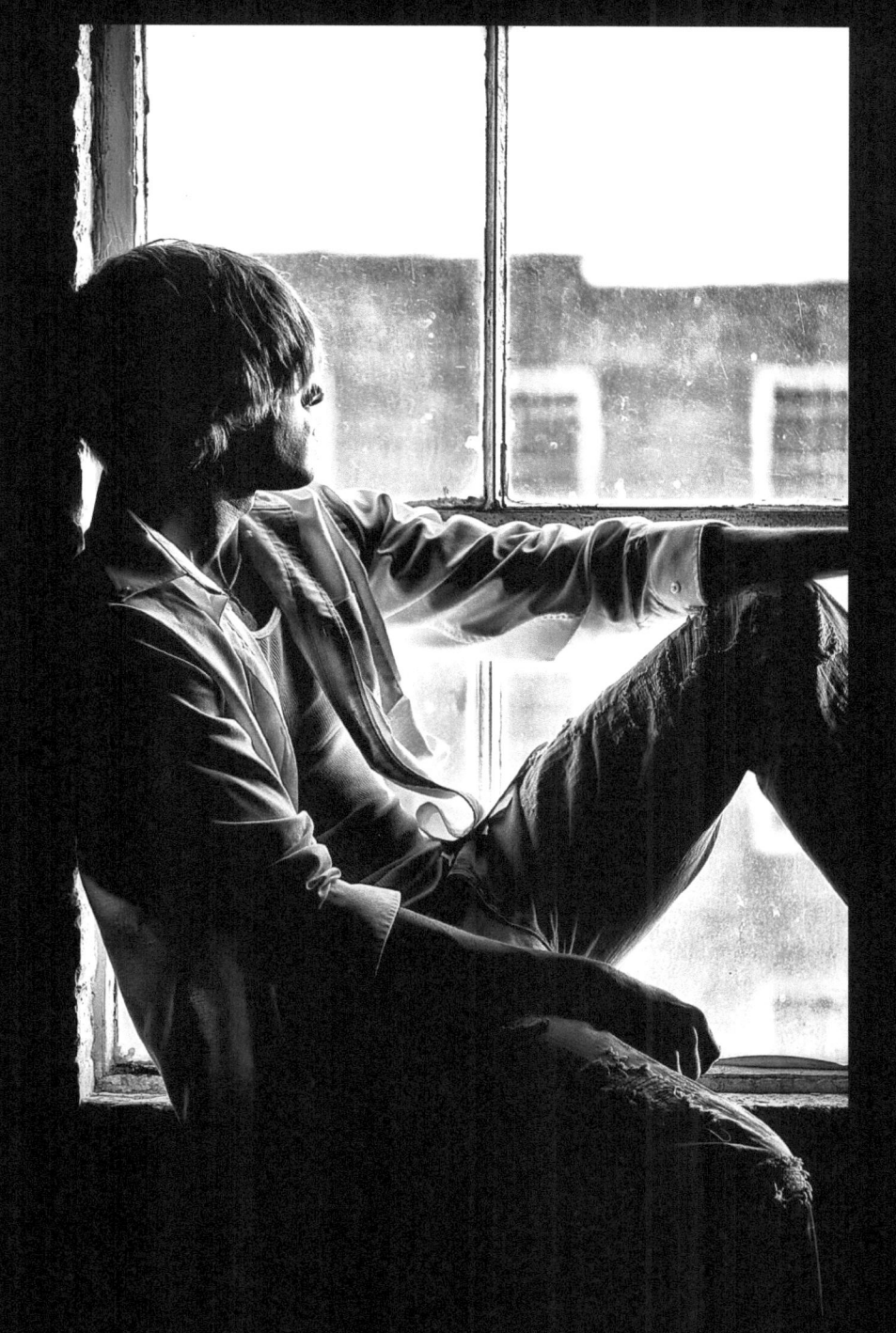

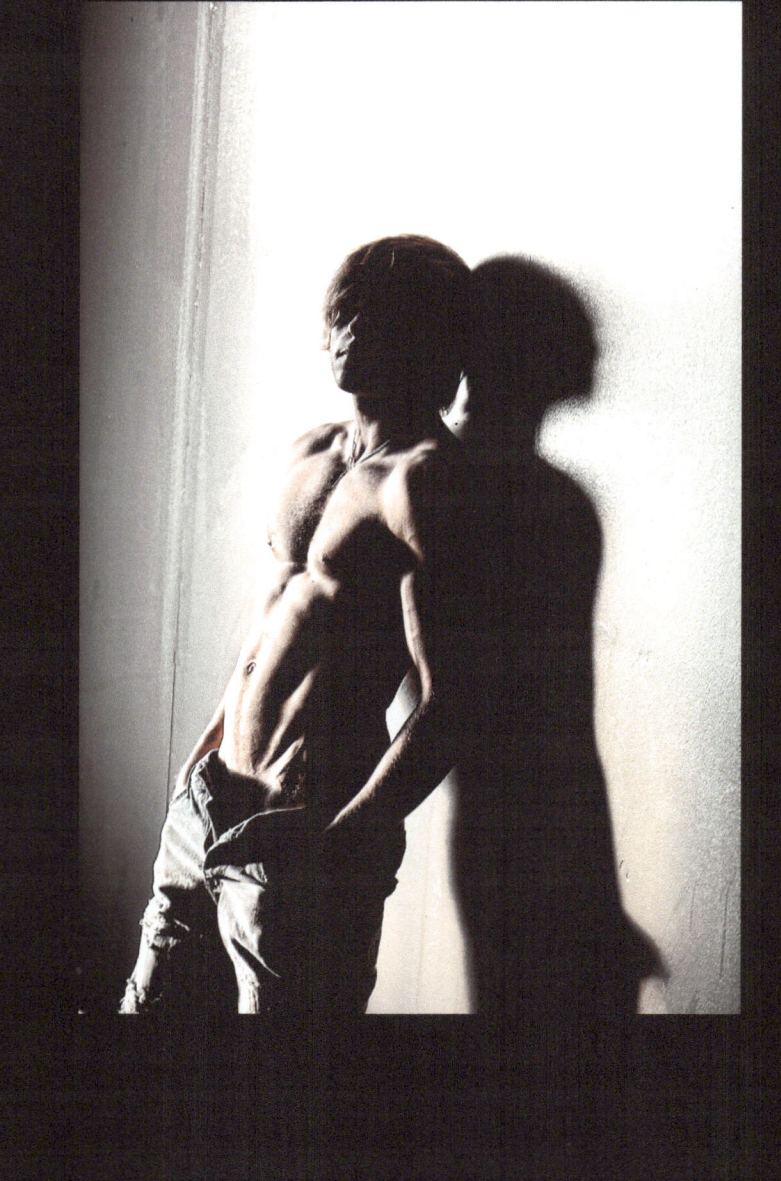

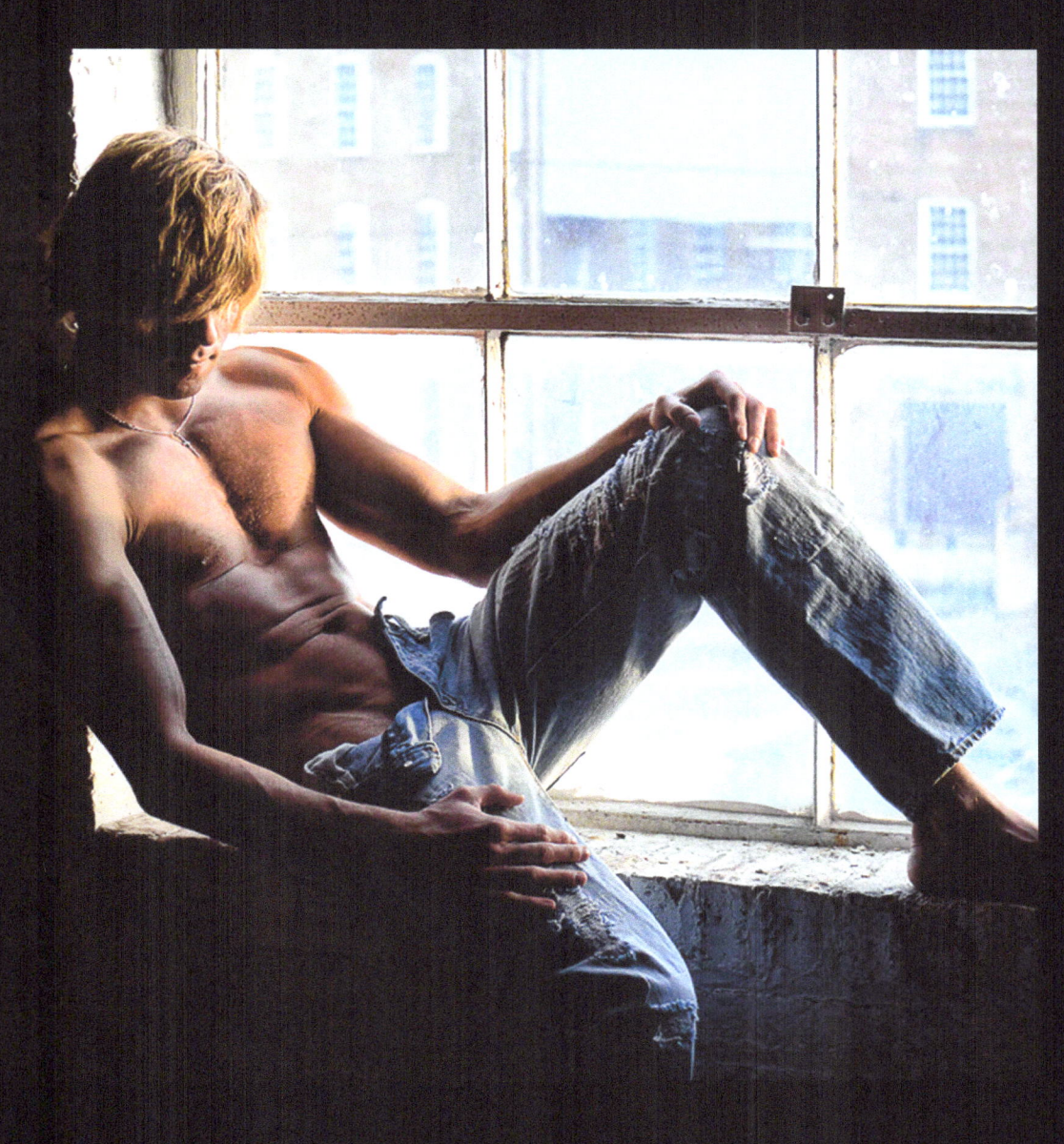

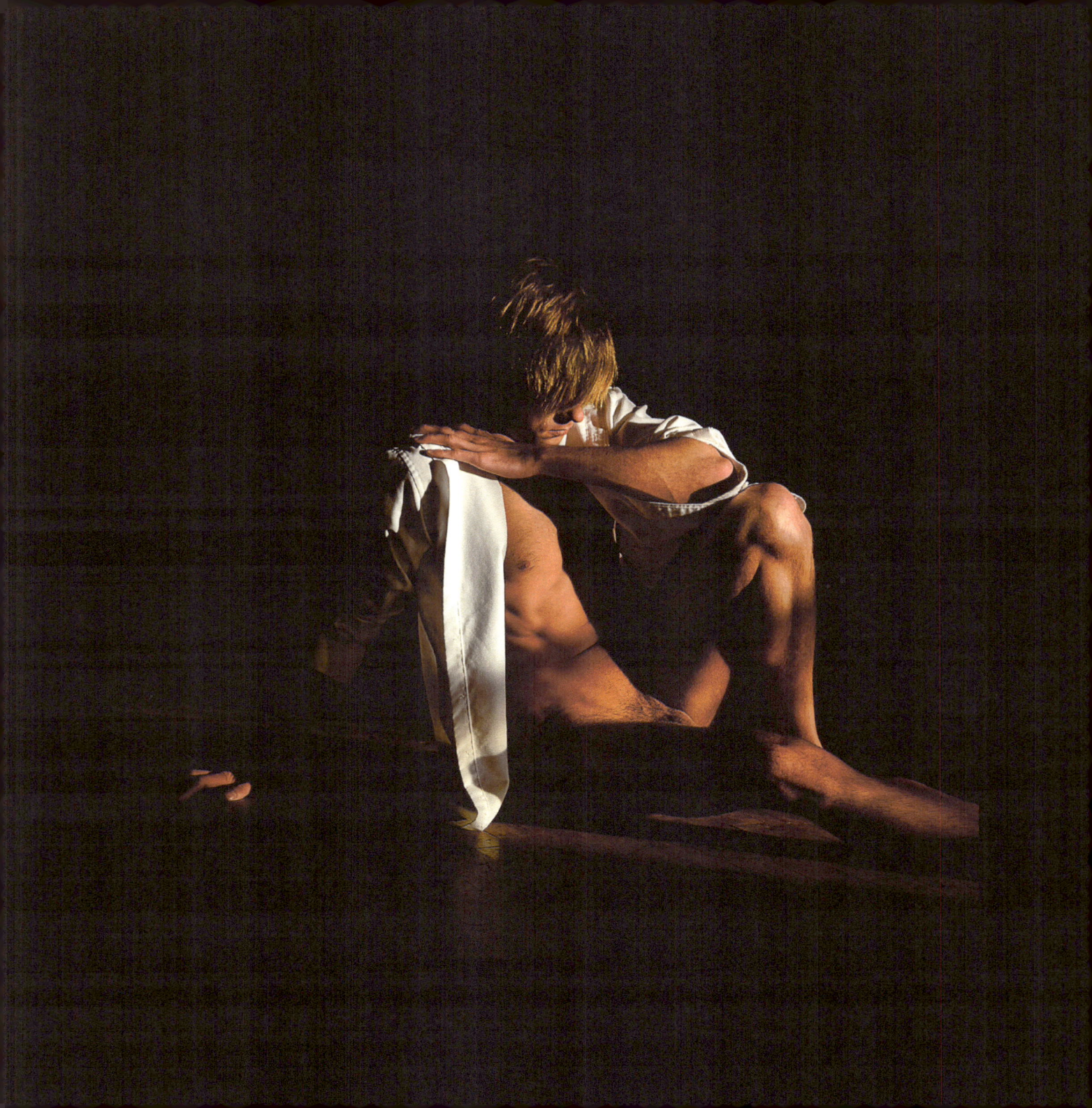

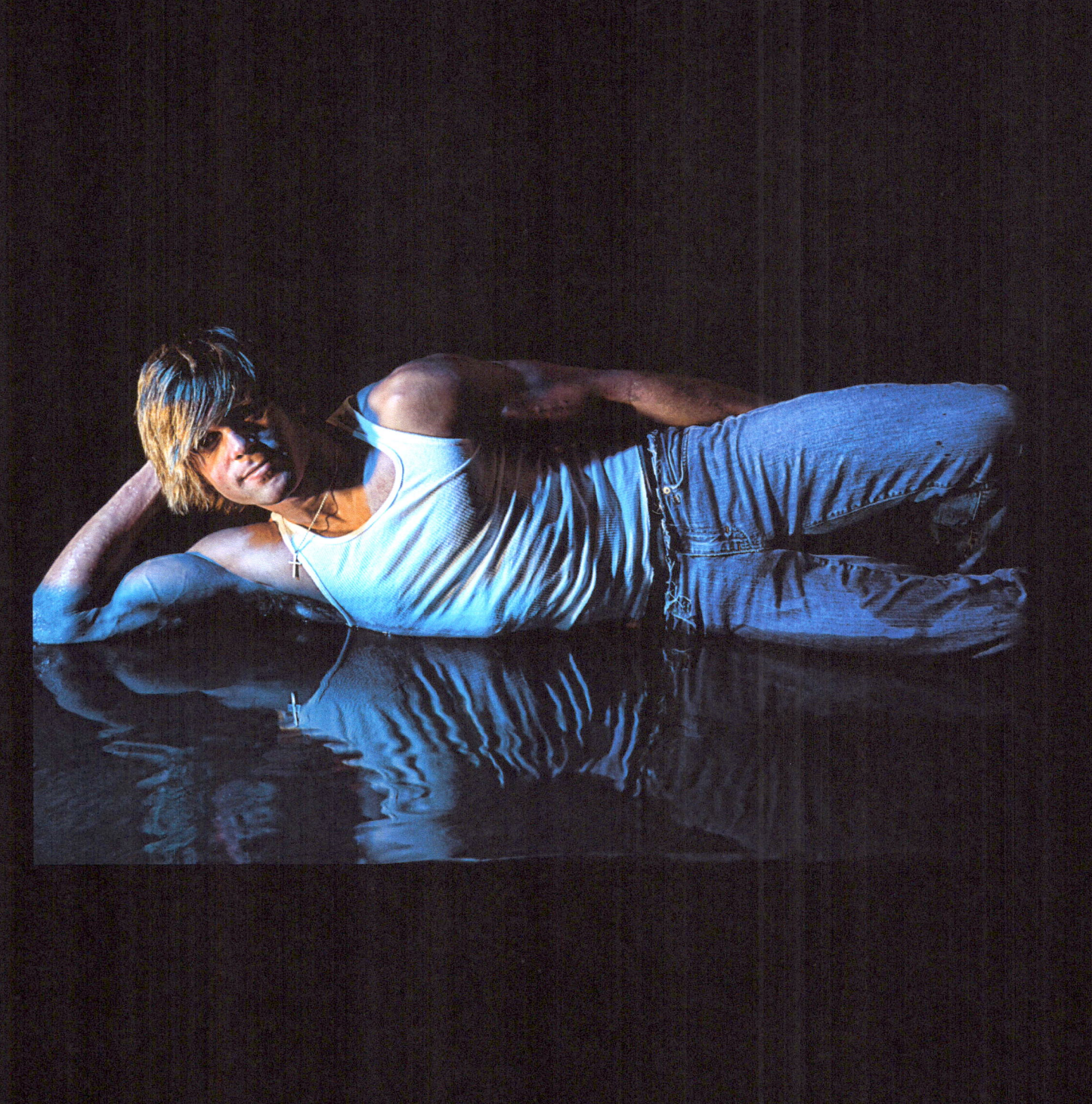

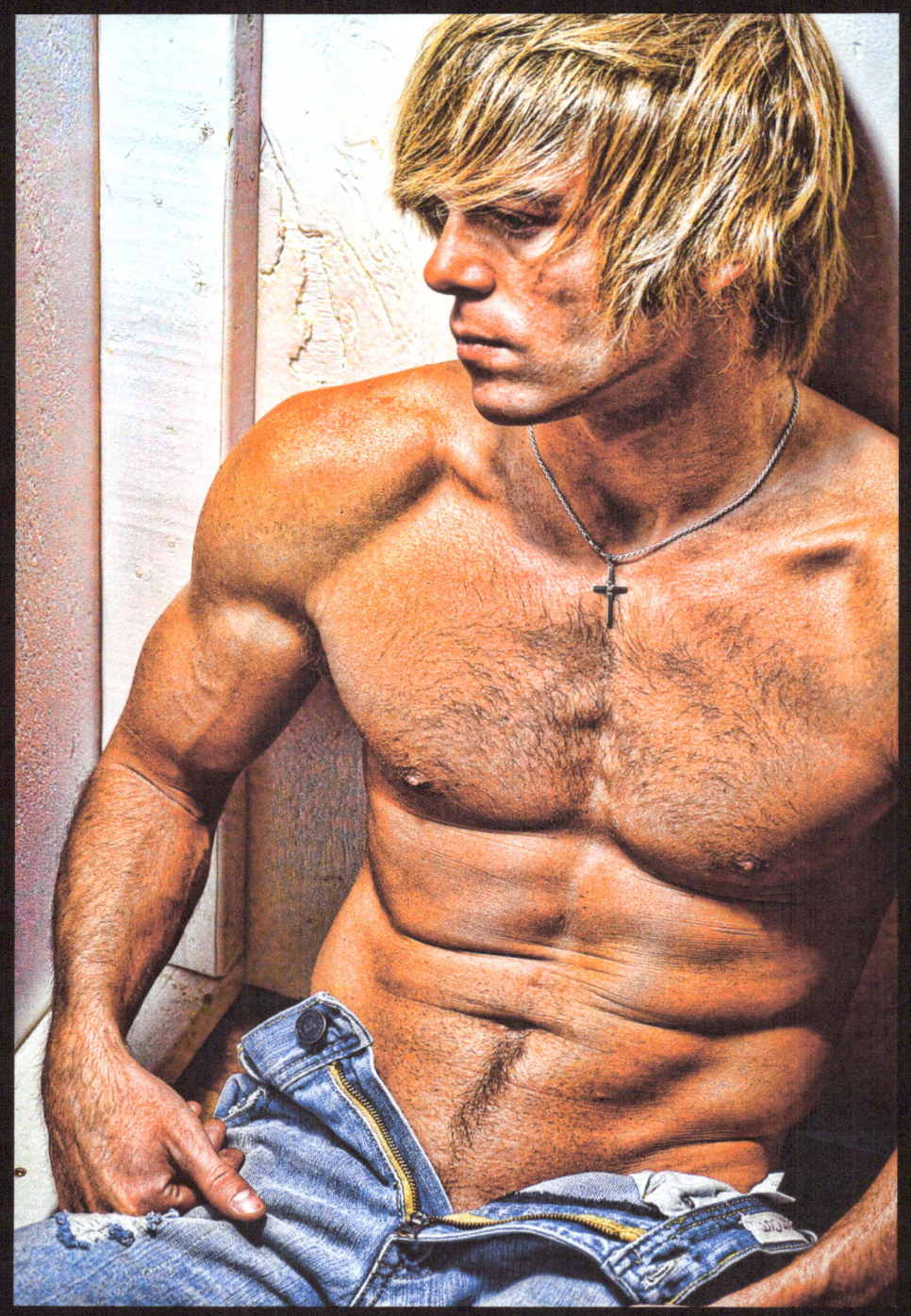

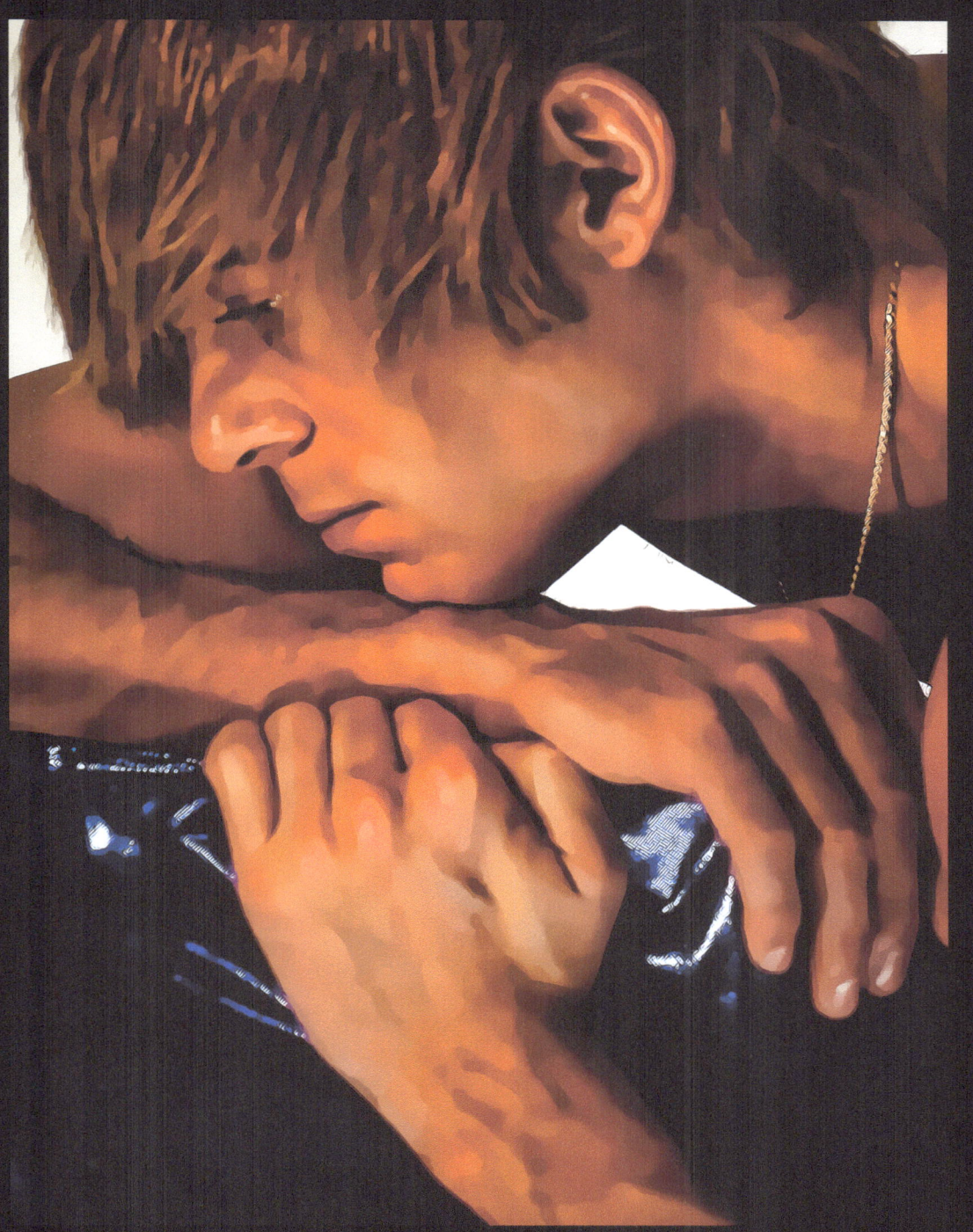

Acknowledgements

I would like to thank each of the "Men" for their great work. It was truly a pleasure working with each of you.

Evertz Saenz
Rafael Luna-Vasquez
Quincey Whittington
Walter Rhone
Scott Vayo
Jake Brennen
Anthony Muncy (Marco Moxie)
Michael Dixon
Patrick Galten

I'd also like to thank Model Mayhem (www.modelmayhem.com) for introducing me to so many of my models.

To see more imagery or to contact the photographer, visit his website at

www.dsimoneauphoto.com

www.ingramcontent.com/pod-product-compliance
Lightning Source LLC
Chambersburg PA
CBHW050739180526
45159CB00003B/1289